DEMANDS OF JUSTICE

Demands of Justice draws on original interviews and archival research to show how global appeals for human rights began in the 1970s to expand the boundaries of the global neighborhood and disseminate new arguments about humane concern and law in direct opposition to human rights violations. Turning a justice lens on human rights practice, Clark argues that human rights practice offers tools that enrich three facets of global justice: transnational expressions of simple concern, the political realization of justice through politics and law, and new but still incomplete approaches to social justice. A key case study explores the origins of Amnesty International's well-known Urgent Action alerts for individuals, as well as temporal change in the use of law in such appeals. A second case study, of Oxfam's adoption of rights language, demonstrates the spread of human rights as a primary way of expressing calls for justice in the world.

ANN MARIE CLARK is a political scientist at Purdue University in West Lafayette, Indiana. She is the author of *Diplomacy of Conscience: Amnesty International and Changing International Human Rights Norms* (2001) and *Sovereignty, Democracy, and Global Civil Society* (2005, with Elisabeth Jay Friedman and Kathryn Hochstetler), and numerous journal articles.

DEMANDS OF JUSTICE

The Creation of a Global Human Rights Practice

ANN MARIE CLARK

Purdue University, Indiana

CAMBRIDGE
UNIVERSITY PRESS

CAMBRIDGE
UNIVERSITY PRESS

University Printing House, Cambridge CB2 8BS, United Kingdom

One Liberty Plaza, 20th Floor, New York, NY 10006, USA

477 Williamstown Road, Port Melbourne, VIC 3207, Australia

314–321, 3rd Floor, Plot 3, Splendor Forum, Jasola District Centre, New Delhi – 110025, India

103 Penang Road, #05–06/07, Visioncrest Commercial, Singapore 238467

Cambridge University Press is part of the University of Cambridge.

It furthers the University's mission by disseminating knowledge in the pursuit of education, learning, and research at the highest international levels of excellence.

www.cambridge.org
Information on this title: www.cambridge.org/9781009098274
DOI: 10.1017/9781009093545

First published 2022

A catalogue record for this publication is available from the British Library.

ISBN 978-1-009-09827-4 Hardback
ISBN 978-1-009-09726-0 Paperback

For Allan and Eve Leadbeater, and the helpers in the world.

To whatever extent contemporary international political life can be said to have a "sense of justice," its language is the language of human rights.

—*Charles Beitz, "Human Rights as a Common Concern"*

CONTENTS

The idea for this book began when I became interested in exploring the use of law in the language of international human rights appeals for individuals in urgent cases, as practiced by Amnesty International (AI). In 2012, I started a research project focusing on AI's "Urgent Action" (UA) alerts from 1975 to 2007, intended to analyze patterns of references to human rights standards in the language of the UA documents. Urgent Action alerts still enable AI supporters to appeal directly to national government officials all over the world for the protection of specific individuals whom AI believes to be threatened by human rights violations.

The project, undertaken with the cooperation and formal agreement of Amnesty International USA as well as informal consultation with staff from AI's headquarters in London, included a plan to create electronic images of more than 20,000 alerts in collaboration with the digital libraries unit at my home university. As part of the research, I also interviewed current and former staffers and volunteers involved in AI's work for people under threat of human rights violations, whom it now calls "individuals at risk." I was increasingly interested in preserving the work of global human rights activists and, as a human rights researcher, I wanted to do what I could to contribute. I had argued in earlier scholarly work that the establishment of human rights law has been a major and lasting achievement of AI and other human rights actors. To pick up on that thread, I was curious to see whether and how global legal norms would appear more frequently in the language of the emergency appeals as time progressed.

It was striking that even as the attention paid to matters of law increased, citations of law did not replace expressions of care. These emergency interventions in situations of real and potential human suffering continued to express simple concern for the people who were threatened. The prevalence of expressions of concern consistently outnumbered periodic references to law and normative obligations of governments. Sophisticated references to justice were largely absent, except for calls that perpetrators be "brought to justice."

Why was this so striking? Perhaps it was because of the simplicity of the actions AI, through the appeals, was asking people to take. Did I expect something grander? On a personal note, I confess that by the time I graduated from college in the early 1980s, although I was very interested in issues related to nonviolent social change, my attitude was rather dismissive toward AI. I had passed by the campus AI table so many times without stopping: How would writing letters for detained individuals abroad change things? The approach seemed unrelated to the cultural and structural change that I saw as necessary at the global level. Thanks to a number of very fine teachers, I had acquired a detailed knowledge of the events that had led to the human rights disasters of the Holocaust in Europe, I had some understanding of the philosophy of law, and was becoming aware of the large-scale harms and injustices then taking place in Central and South America. I would not have predicted, though, that human rights in Latin America and the work of human rights organizations like AI would later become focal points of my scholarly research. When I did take that turn, the research I did on AI concentrated on its role in the creation of global legal norms to protect against torture, disappearances, and political killings, not the endless stream of appeals for individuals that AI had generated over decades.

So, in encountering the texts of the UAs several years ago, I began to reassess some of my expectations in the long view of human rights work as work for justice at the global level. I had seen human rights as contributing to justice through change in global legal norms and social expectations for the behavior of states. Was the expression of human concern also a part of justice? What about the references that did not appear, such as invocations of social justice, which still challenge existing models of civil and political rights action? What could these texts tell us about work for justice in the face of injustice? Early in the project I also learned that Oxfam, the anti-poverty organization, had begun to use human rights language in its work for social justice, as had other development sector groups. I began to realize that these questions about paths to justice were bigger than the matter of law in the texts of a single organization.

Such questions remain external to many empirical studies of international relations actors, yet they began to appear integral to a topic I have long been interested in: How do people without much more than compelling language move world politics toward justice? To situate the UA texts in such a context, I chose to turn to political theorists and philosophers for help. This book contains some of the research I had envisioned on the growth of references to law, but the book also situates that in the context of a set of ways that justice could be pursued. What did the appeals sent from that campus AI group's letter-writing table mean for just outcomes? How have encounters, figurative and real, between would-be global helpers and persons at risk changed the practice of human rights? Why was rights language adopted by development organizations like Oxfam as they have pursued economic justice? And in the world of international and transnational politics, what tools do human rights offer for justice? The first-person accounts, textual data, and analysis included in the following pages represent an effort to answer these questions.

The Approach of the Book

I argue in this book that the human rights movement has created a resilient practice for seeking global justice. Global human rights advocates have devised tools that can be used over and over to seek justice, not only to fight against injustice. The tools include a network for information sharing, a language of appeal in urgent situations, a structure of norms and legal accountability, and even new understandings of rights. The tools of rights advocacy, however they were invented, have been honed in use.

To address injustice by power holders, human rights norms draw on compelling notions of justice, freedom, and equality for all persons. Although widely endorsed, the rules and norms of human rights compete with other incentives and goals held by governments and other powerful actors in a changing international system. An underlying theme of the book, then, is that rights advocacy has historically expanded the scope of its ambitions to meet the demands of justice.

Human rights ideas may converge on justice in their form and application, but they are not equivalent to justice. Even as human rights comes to mind when people talk about justice, rights advocates have constantly debated among themselves how best to adapt their tools, or devise new ones, to suit new issues that have become new human rights problems. The push and pull between justice and human rights is, to a great extent, a mutually constitutive process. The rule of law and respect for the rights of individuals already comprise widely shared understandings of how procedural justice should operate in politics. Beyond those normative achievements, when there is a new political, social, or economic issue that can be defined as a human rights problem, it seems that modern conceptions of justice require that it be recognized and addressed, no matter the past successes of the human rights framework.

As I will show, reconciling the tension between justice ideals and the practical political problems faced by human rights actors is challenging but potentially productive. Justice is a high and complex standard for the conduct of politics. Justice places demands on politics, and therefore on human rights, that the practice cannot always fulfill.

Further, justice is a moving target. Social and political understandings of justice are subject to change, as are views regarding appropriate and achievable human rights goals. If human rights advocates are at all reflective, they realize that in a fluid political context, they can only act imperfectly to promote, respect, and fulfill human rights standards.

The recognition that human rights work nearly always falls short of justice ideals is evident in academic studies of the human rights movement. In my own field of political science, for example, studies of the influence that human rights organizations have achieved globally have also raised questions about how and whether strategic choices – part of the interest-based politics that activists must negotiate – undermine the loftiness of their cause. Among other social scientists and historians who study human rights, a similar trend is apparent. In all of these studies, failures of human rights actors to live up to stated ideals while engaging in political action come into view. What to make of the gap? My answer is that the failures are real, but that many of the successes are real, too. In this book, I center on points when new formulations of human rights advocacy became possible as a response to the gap between justice and politics. In the cases represented here, advocates working through global NGOs began to recognize the need for new potential avenues to a more just world.

As the book shows, devising and implementing practical action to approach an ideal is a central feature of human rights activism. As researchers, unless we also try to understand the actors' contemporaneous reasons for human rights action, we miss important drivers of change in global politics. By setting the emergence of human rights language and practice in the context of theoretical features of justice, I bring focus to three identifiable changes in human rights practices since the 1960s: a move from generalized humanitarian-style care to organized human rights action for individuals; from case-by-case action to a structure of human rights law; and from addressing civil and political harms to the recognition of structural economic and social injustices as rights issues.

A Nod to Activists

My research for the book has allowed me to meet people whom I have come to admire greatly. As they demonstrate, resting when encountering limits – or when recognizing accomplishments – is not the usual habit of human rights advocates. Allowing conceptions of justice to shape a study of rights-based advocacy elevates the continuing commitment of (often sparingly) paid staffers and unpaid volunteers, member-participants, and others with the capacity to assist, acting together to address wrongs to fellow human beings. They would be the first to say that they should not be idealized, and they are right, but we can learn from their examples. Advocacy efforts require skill and a deep persistence that may not see immediate results. The logistics of global advocacy pose considerable challenges as well, requiring among other things that those who occupy a relatively safe position learn to build effective solidarity with people whose lives and livelihoods are directly threatened by human rights violations. Aside from helping us learn something about justice-seeking, my hope is that this book also helps to preserve some noteworthy first-person accounts of how things once were, and to emphasize that creative use of old and new tools of justice is still called for today.

ACKNOWLEDGMENTS

This book has taken time to come to fruition, and I have many people to thank.

For comments on the book manuscript, I especially want to thank Geoff Dancy, Kathryn Sikkink, and Beth Simmons, who generously agreed to read and discuss a first draft of the book in 2019. They provided serious yet supportive feedback that helped me improve the manuscript and move it to completion. Geoff kindly read portions of a later version as well. Comments from two anonymous reviewers were enormously helpful, and it has been a pleasure to work with John Haslam of Cambridge University Press.

Others who have commented on parts of the research include Shareen Hertel, Aaron Hoffman, Melissa LaBonte, James A. McCann, Kurt Mills, Mintao Nie, Leigh Raymond, Christian Reus-Smit, Mary (Molly) Scudder, and Jack Snyder. Papers were presented at the Columbia University Human Rights Seminar; the Moral Revolutions: Institutional and Ideational Dimensions conference at Nanyang Technological University, Singapore; the *Millennium* conference, Out of the Ivory Tower: Weaving the Theories and Practice of International Relations, at the London School of Economics; the International Studies Association Workshop on Human Rights and Justice in The Hague; the Purdue Human Rights Program Research Workshop; the annual meeting of the Law and Society Association; and the Department of Political Science at the University of Vermont. Thanks to Elazar Barkan and Yasmine Ergas of the Institute for the Study of Human Rights at Columbia University, where I spent two semesters as a visiting scholar.

Infinite appreciation to my dear writing accountability colleagues: Anne Foegen, Jane Goodman, and Molly Scudder. For additional collegial hospitality and conversation, thanks to Rosalee Clawson, Michael Freeman, Kathryn Hochstetler, Cherie Maestas, Anja Mihr, Keith Shimko, and Swati Srivastava.

The documents project that enabled me to gather the textual data on the UAs was undertaken under a formal agreement with Amnesty International USA, and I would like to thank Samir Goswami, then of Amnesty International USA, for his initial interest and support when the idea for the project was hatched, as well as Zeke Johnson, Michael McClintock, and Jamie Wood, also of Amnesty International USA. I thank Pamela Graham, director of the Center for Human Rights Documentation and Research at Columbia University, the site of Amnesty International USA's archives, for helpful consultation. Ellen Moore, whose story appears in Chapter 4 in the account of the earliest days of the UA network, also helped to found Amnesty International USA's archives, which began at the University of Colorado at Boulder before moving to Columbia University. A conversation with Ellen during a conference on human rights archives and documentation in 2007 at Columbia planted the seed of an idea for research on the old UA documents.

A core group of excellent graduate assistants formed the research team that coded thirty-three years' worth of AI's UA texts. I would like to thank the original members of the graduate student research team, all of whom have since finished their PhD studies and moved on to their own careers: Ñusta Carranza Ko, Mintao Nie, Zuzana Ringlerova, Dan Sinh Nguyen, and Bi Zhao. For additional assistance, I thank Anna Kowalski, Elis Vllasi, Elle Rochford, Fanqing Liu, Mary Christine Aylwan and Sarah King. Funding from Purdue University's Office of the Vice President for Research made the digitizing work possible through an Enhancing Research in the Humanities and the Arts grant. Paul J. Bracke, then the associate dean of Libraries at Purdue University, joined me as co-principal investigator on that project. An R^2 grant from the Purdue University's Office of the Provost provided additional resources and time for research and writing.

Librarians and archivists are sometimes underappreciated by fellow academics. My colleagues in Purdue Libraries provided essential collaboration in this project. Additional thanks are due to the International Institute for Social History staff in Amsterdam, the site of AI's global archives, and the archives and manuscripts staff of the Bodleian Libraries in Oxford, where Oxfam GB's papers are housed.

Paul J. Bracke facilitated the project as a point person in Purdue Libraries, helping me to organize the researcher–practitioner–library collaboration that allowed us to work with Amnesty International USA to digitize the series of UA documents not only for my research but for an eventual public-facing e-collection of the documents that is to be housed at Purdue. Archivists at AI's International Secretariat in London, Fiona Bolt and Bryony Hooper, shared files and metadata that greatly facilitated progress.

I am grateful to several other members of Purdue Libraries staff for invaluable assistance. Matt Riehle, lead web applications developer of Purdue Libraries IT, my main contact for the technical aspects of the project, has been unfailingly helpful and good natured, even during the most frustrating parts of the project. I can't thank him enough. Cliff Harrison and Amy Barton offered additional technical assistance.

As I conclude this long list of thank you notes, I reflect with gratitude on the friendship and care that I have experienced in my personal life. I especially thank Kathryn Elliott (and Tim, Ralph, and Hope), Lisa Goffman and Bill Saxton, Barbara LaFever, Allan and Eve Leadbeater, Marybeth Lorbiecki Mataya, John B. Stephens, and Beth Strickland for various forms of love, friendship, and encouragement as I was working on this project. Personal thanks also to Fabian Arnaldo, Wasima Hassan, Aleksey Madan, Marie Pennanen, and Debbie Sparks.

Lastly, the constancy of my wonderful family means the world: Lucy Clark, Emily Clark, Brad McLemore, George, Elizabeth, Will, and Sophie Clark, and all of my Chicago *famiglia*, with fond memories of Mary Ann. All my love to Jay, for years of abiding partnership and joy.

Introduction

Human Rights Advocacy and the Demands of Justice

In 1971, human rights violations had begun to intensify in Brazil. Suspected political opponents of the government were being abducted or arrested, brutally tortured, and sometimes killed by agents of the military government. Torture would usually happen quickly, either before or immediately after arrest. In London, Amnesty International's (AI's) new researcher on Brazil, Tracy Ulltveit-Moe, was receiving blunt feedback from her Brazilian contacts. It was apparent that AI's existing methods were too slow and too narrowly focused to address the scope and nature of violations in Brazil. In a small, weekend meeting among a handful of colleagues and Brazil observers, Ulltveit-Moe proposed that AI organize immediate alerts instead. Amnesty International could contact members as soon as information was confirmed, asking them to write immediately to government officials on behalf of individuals at severe risk of harm. This "Urgent Action" (UA) process, most likely the first of its kind, was tested in AI's first Campaign against Torture and was eventually adopted as a permanent part of AI's working methods. At nearly the same time, AI began efforts at the United Nations (UN) to develop international human rights law and reinforce international legal arguments to support human rights. The language of thousands of UA alerts issued since reflects the transnational expression of ordinary care in the face of threat, supplemented by arguments based on the emerging global legal structure of human rights.

Two decades later, in a different sector of global advocacy, anti-poverty groups like Oxfam had become expert at delivering material resources to grassroots projects in the Global South. Oxfam's fundraising base included a loyal membership in Britain and other wealthy countries. At the same time, the perceived failure of prevailing models of international economic development to support economic and social equity for people in the countries Oxfam served had become a major justice concern. Encounters with unprecedented numbers of fellow nongovernmental organizations (NGOs) attending the 1992 UN Conference on Environment and Development, the 1993 UN World Conference on Human Rights, the 1995 Fourth World Conference on Women, and the other post-Cold War conferences of that decade on human habitat and social equity brought home the urgency of reconciling global inequity with the rights of people living in poverty. Although few human rights groups had yet incorporated social justice into their working mandates, Oxfam and numerous other development-sector groups began to raise broader themes of human rights as part of their social justice advocacy. For Oxfam, the shift in approach was preceded by careful study of the issues and an intense effort to shift the charity-based culture shared by many of its grassroots members and – through support for human rights – to uphold the political agency of people in the countries that they served.

These two anecdotes are drawn from more detailed accounts presented in the chapters that follow. They presage the themes of this book. Every day, human rights advocates across the globe muster concrete efforts to demand justice in the face of terrible injustice. Human rights activists are usually much less powerful than the forces behind the injustices that they seek to keep at bay, an imbalance magnified in the context of changing repressive techniques. Achieving even a measure of success requires the development of new tools for action and the persistent refinement of those tools. The Oxfam case demonstrates a convergence of human rights advocacy tools, including rights language, as part of work for social justice in sectors of transnational activity beyond human rights. In both cases, the shortcomings of support for distant neighbors arise in debates among agents of change whose circumstances and politics may differ from those of their neighbors. In this way, even as advocates demand justice of those in power, justice also makes demands on human rights actors themselves.

The material presented in this book provides an invitation to think about how international human rights work intersects with broader ideas about what global justice is, and how to achieve it. My working hypothesis is that human rights advocates have developed a lasting set of tools for pursuing justice, amounting to a justice-seeking practice. To support the hypothesis requires seeking evidence: What are the relevant components of justice; and what can be observed about whether and how human rights practices fulfill the promises of justice?

The evidence I present is linked to three components of global justice. My account is compatible with a nonideal conception of justice, in which actors seek to make social arrangements "more just" rather than perfectly just. A nonideal conception captures the circumstances that human rights actors find themselves in when they engage in politics. The first aspect of justice is the development of Samaritan-like care and concern for the conditions that prevent people from living free and full lives. Human rights actors linked human rights action to a notion of care that broadens the appropriate subject of care to a global neighborhood. The second aspect of justice pertains to an institutional structure in which legal norms can (but do not always) serve as independent standards of justice. Human rights actors generated globally relevant forms of argument based on law and concern that have transformed rights into a language of legal justice and accountability that can be employed in appeals to power holders. The third aspect of justice calls for the integration of social justice into politics as human rights standards upholding economic, social, and cultural equity, including gender and racial inclusion. It can be observed now that human rights actors are increasingly using a language of social justice, but repertoires of action for this aspect of justice are still emerging. In the third part of the study, I focus on observing human rights and anti-poverty actors' translation and sharing of ways to implement social justice. The adoption of rights-based approaches by organizations in the development sector testifies to the usefulness of tools developed by human rights groups, but also to areas where justice has to be a common enterprise.

Human Rights Work as a Justice-Seeking Practice

The view of human rights work presented in this book offers an interactive and incremental account of the pursuit of justice that is grounded in the observation of the regular activities advocates have developed to support international human rights norms in world politics. In this study, I refer to their efforts as human rights work, or human rights practice.

Emanuel Adler and Vincent Pouliot define practices in international relations as "socially meaningful patterns of action" that "pertain to world politics."[1] Practices are "intersubjective," according to Mervyn Frost and Silviya Lechner: they are created, maintained, and potentially altered through social interaction and the reasons actors give for what they do.[2] The intersubjective aspects of human rights practice appear in the ways that the individuals and organizations involved in the practice revise their goals, alter their approaches, and change their arguments as they seek to improve behavioral respect for

---

[1] Emanuel Adler and Vincent Pouliot, "International Practices," *International Theory* 3, no. 1 (2011): 4, 6. See also *International Practices* (Cambridge: Cambridge University Press, 2011).

[2] Mervyn Frost and Silviya Lechner, "Understanding International Practices from the Internal Point of View," *Journal of International Political Theory* 12, no. 3 (2015): 308–311.

4

human rights. Human rights practice is "both discursive and political," according to Charles Beitz.[3]

In this study, I have concentrated on the contributions to human rights practice made by human rights advocates in support of persons affected by human rights violations, thus highlighting a part, not the whole, of human rights as a comprehensive practice in global politics. Although human rights is a global practice, human rights practitioners operate at many levels of politics and in many locales,[4] involving a range of actors beyond NGOs, including those within and outside of nation-states, intergovernmental organizations, and even corporations. In observing and theorizing how human rights action has contributed to aspects of justice, the repertoires of action developed by human rights advocates can also be understood as a particular kind of justice-seeking practice. This cross-fertilization of human rights and justice-seeking is confirmed in the case study of how and why Oxfam took up human rights in its work for justice in the face of poverty.

Like other practices, human rights practice gives rise to "a rich and ongoing set of claims and counter-claims, descriptions and counter-descriptions, . . . about what is happening within the global practice of states."[5] Other "patterns of action" that comprise human rights practice, but are not a major focus of this book, include the politics surrounding the obligations posed by human rights norms; efforts to

---

[3] Charles R. Beitz, *The Idea of Human Rights* (Oxford: Oxford University Press, 2009), 9.

[4] According to Adler and Pouliot, whether a practice is "global, international, transnational, regional, organizational, substate, local, etc. – is itself a matter of practice: defining what counts as an international practice and what does not is best left to practitioners themselves in their actual performance of world politics" (Adler and Pouliot, "International Practices," 6).

[5] Frost and Lechner, "Understanding International Practices from the Internal Point of View," 313.

articulate how human rights principles apply to businesses and other non-state entities; the activities of intergovernmental organizations related to human rights monitoring and reporting; the activities of the groups and individuals who do the reporting; and rulings on human rights obligations and accountability in courts of law at various levels. Citing the increasing authority of human rights globally, Frost and Lechner see human rights as one of two "major global practices in international relations."[6] The second is the practice of sovereignty, an interesting pairing since human rights politics and sovereignty politics are so often at odds.[7]

Research Strategy

Human rights speaks to the conduct of international politics in ways directly related to ideas about justice. The purview of human rights activism has been defined and redefined over time as human rights claims have targeted different kinds of justice goals. International human rights advocates, reacting to perceived injustices that they labeled as human rights violations, developed a set of approaches that comprise distinct methods of understanding and working for justice. Although advocacy work is a flawed reflection of ideal justice, conceptualizing human rights advocacy as an effort to do the political work that justice requires is a theoretically productive way to interpret the trajectory of human rights practices, and it is the framework for the arguments that I advance in this book.

Rather than make this argument only in the abstract, I explore the observable implications of human rights as work for justice. This

---

[6] Ibid., 312.

[7] See, e.g., Elisabeth Jay Friedman, Kathryn Hochstetler, and Ann Marie Clark, *Sovereignty, Democracy, and Global Civil Society: State-Society Relations at UN World Conferences* (Albany: State University of New York Press, 2005).

includes interventions that ordinary people – as individuals and in organizations and movements – have made on behalf of human rights globally over decades. In so doing, I return with a deliberate focus to the beginnings of some of the rights-based appeals that we may take for granted now: how they were invented, chosen, implemented, and themselves challenged in the effort to achieve more justice.

The study digs deep into the work of two large, global NGOs: AI and, to a lesser extent, Oxfam. Amnesty International originated many of the human rights advocacy techniques used widely today. A focus on AI offers the opportunity to observe changing approaches to human rights advocacy in a single organization. Oxfam is even older than AI and, similarly, has evolved in its approach to aid, and to economic justice at the global level. The two organizations are also comparable in that, historically, both have encouraged supporters to participate actively in rights advocacy and aid.

To observe change in human rights practices, I focus on AI in Chapters 4 and 5. As the oldest membership-based human rights NGO, AI was a model and prototype for global human rights advocacy. The invention of its UA approach demonstrates an early shift in its practice that was motivated in large part by the recognition that it needed to do more to address the severe rights violations it was encountering in its work. The texts of its UA alerts provide a picture of the increasing incorporation of legal norms in the language of appeals for the human rights of individuals over time. The UA approach, and the language of its appeals, provides a focal point for the emergence of some basic human rights approaches to justice: the transnational extension of concern to address how governments treat individuals; and the consolidation of that concern with law and argument, two elements that brought human rights into the political realm.

Oxfam, the focus of Chapter 6, has a pedigree like that of AI. It, too, is a long-lived, membership-based NGO, but has focused on poverty relief, not human rights. The study of Oxfam's adoption of rights-based language to oppose global poverty highlights some of the challenges posed by unjust patterns of social and economic development. In the 1990s, Oxfam and other actors in the development sector began to call for human rights as a path to more justice in national and international economic development policies.

Amnesty International developed the Urgent Action network along with a broader legal and human rights approach in the 1970s in response to a changing human rights environment and, also, by the demands of justice: to do right, they needed to "do more." Later, as Oxfam began to see need for political engagement in order for the poor to receive justice, it turned to rights. For both NGOs, internal debates prompted by their encounters with the world and with injustice drove decisions to develop new ways to use human rights as tools of justice.

A background premise of the case studies, reinforced by the accounts presented in the book, is that advocacy NGOs and their staffers and members are oriented toward making a difference in the causes that they care about. In the practice of human rights advocates, we see calls for case-by-case relief, procedural skill, and active engagement with new legal approaches to systematize responses that will bring not only relief but also successful monitoring and accountability. As recounted in the book, the human rights actors I encountered were keenly aware of the limitations of their work, but also keenly interested in contributing to just outcomes. To learn about their efforts as they created and worked out an emerging practice oriented toward justice, I have relied on research interviews and archival materials as well as secondary sources. I spoke with current and former staffers, as well as volunteers, to learn more about how the people involved in developing and carrying out early, pathbreaking human rights–oriented action thought about their efforts at the time.[8] Frost and Lechner refer to

---

[8] Interview research was carried out as approved by the Purdue University Human Protection Program. Protocol no. 1304013487, "Transnational Work for Justice" (Ann

this actor-centered theoretical approach as uncovering the "internal point of view."[9] What problems were these actors trying to solve, and how did they envision the work? I chose such an approach for two reasons: First, it enables the preservation of first-person accounts of important innovations in human rights practice; and second, it supports an exploration of the strengths and challenges of human rights practice as a form of action oriented toward justice.

Outline of the Book

In Chapter 2, I briefly review the links between human rights and selected treatments of justice in the scholarly literature. Drawing on this literature, I identify the elements of the search for justice in international politics that are illuminated when we observe the dynamics of human rights work. In Chapter 3, I then theorize how three aspects of justice have been foundational, at different times, to the human rights movement: (1) a justice of care extended to a global neighborhood; (2) a culture of argument incorporating law in appeals to political authority; and (3) social justice. Each is addressed in different aspects of human rights practice, and each has its own repertoire, or set of tools, for justice-seeking. Although they overlap, they are also time-ordered and somewhat cumulative. Transnational human rights advocacy has historically invoked both care and law to specify rights demands. The third aspect, social justice, has presented more of a challenge for traditional human rights practices, despite the fact that the framers of the Universal Declaration of Human Rights in 1948 included economic, social, and cultural rights.

Marie Clark, Principal Investigator, approval date May 7, 2013, with ongoing renewal).

[9] Frost and Lechner, "Understanding International Practices from the Internal Point of View."

Chapters 4–6 explore how human rights practice has informed and been informed by the components of justice theorized in Chapter 3. Each focuses on separate, observable features of human rights action. Chapter 4 tells the story of the evolution of UA appeals for the individual, as developed by AI in the 1970s. It covers the establishment of the Urgent Action network in the USA and Germany, as well as how the network has operated more recently, relying on original interviews with a number of staff and individuals involved in AI's UA work. Their stories are fascinating as first-person accounts. They are also theoretically relevant to understanding the pursuit of justice because they demonstrate the importance of sustained effort and well-honed skills, complemented by transnationally oriented concern. The narratives in Chapter 4 demonstrate how what I call active care has sustained human rights efforts, and also how it led advocates to recognize shortcomings and revise their approaches to advocacy and solidarity, even in the earliest days.

Chapter 5 analyzes the discursive content of the UA texts as forms of appeal over a thirty-three–year period. The UA texts were sent to a network of AI members willing to write messages opposing reported mistreatment of individuals in government custody via direct messages to governments. Because the texts offer a decades-long record of a single form of activism, they also serve as data that can help us gauge changes in the language and practice of rights advocacy. As global legal norms of human rights were adopted by nation-states and could themselves be used as compelling points of reference for moral action, evidence shows that legal arguments entered the texts more frequently. At the same time, however, reasoning based on expression of simple concern for individual situations continued to appear in the documents.

Chapter 6 considers how rights have been used to address economic and social justice. It switches focus to global advocacy by social and economic justice actors who turned toward what is commonly called a rights-based approach to development. The case study in this chapter traces how and why Oxfam recast its goals as a set of what it called "basic rights." Oxfam's adoption of human rights language in its aid and economic justice advocacy work was taken at the same time that traditional human rights NGOs hotly debated how and whether to take up economic, social, and cultural rights more directly.

Finally, Chapter 7 discusses the book's findings and sums up lessons of the study for the conduct of international politics. I argue that human rights work has contributed significant, politically embedded global resources for justice-seeking. The resources as they now exist support active transnational concern for individuals in diverse circumstances, offer a language of appeals for issues related to justice, and inspire the search for more justice in global politics.

2

Human Rights and Justice in Global Politics

As a form of justice work, human rights advocacy has fostered transnational care and support for people in situations of immediate physical threat from their own governments. Human rights advocates have also helped to establish political accountability for such harms, by strengthening moral and legal standards that critique the actions of power holders and build upon their legal obligations. These two contributions – care and a politics of rights – have roots in how people think about justice, and lie at the core of human rights as a way of pursuing global justice. In addition, human rights are increasingly being employed as part of the language of social justice concerns in the pursuit of economic, social, and cultural equity.

Observing changes in human rights practices offers a way of learning about practical support for justice in this world. Human rights principles address the just treatment of individuals not only as subjects of political authority but more broadly as persons due equal respect and concern. Although nation-states are the principal addressees and authors of formal human rights standards in international law, much human rights advocacy has been carried out through transnational work by nongovernmental organizations (NGOs) and individual members of civil society. The earliest and most prominent efforts at direct, transnational action for individuals were initiated by Amnesty International (AI; also known as Amnesty), founded in 1961. Since then, AI has been joined by many other human rights NGOs in the pursuit of political change organized around human rights principles.

In the course of their work, human rights advocates have created new approaches and adapted older practices for seeking justice at home and abroad. Their work has contributed to shifts in international human rights norms as legal and social standards for how nation-states and other power holders should behave, which advocates then invoke on behalf of people threatened by human rights violations. Those shifts have included responses to nation-states' changing techniques of repression; the creation and use of new legal standards of human rights; the application of human rights to nongovernmental entities such as business interests and armed groups; and changing social standards, in the sense that advocates' own ideas of what their relevant tasks should be have evolved. Human rights workers have learned how to use appeals to human concern, law, and equality to try to protect individuals in situations of injustice.

Such activities exemplify what Beitz theorizes as the essential qualities of human rights as a practice. First, human rights establish "institutional protections against standard threats" to "urgent individual interests."[1] Second, human rights set obligations and expectations for states.[2] Third, human rights are "matters of international concern," meaning that human rights principles undergird reasons for action by "outside agents" when states fail to act in situations of likely harm.[3] Allen Buchanan offers a more detailed list of what is included in the practice of human rights: human rights treaty processes, the activities of international organizations and international courts, the work of international human rights NGOs, the efforts of individuals, foreign aid conditionality based on human rights criteria, and more.[4]

My main focus will be on the features of human rights practice that make up the tools that global human rights advocates, as "outside agents," have developed. The qualities of international human rights just mentioned help us to understand how and why human rights

---

[1] Beitz, *The Idea of Human Rights*, 111. [2] Ibid., 113. [3] Ibid., 115.

[4] Allen E. Buchanan, *The Heart of Human Rights* (Oxford: Oxford University Press, 2013), 6. Buchanan focuses on human rights in the international legal system. There are substantial differences among Beitz, Buchanan, and other political theorists who discuss human rights, but it is not necessary to review them here.

principles not only function as norms of behavior for states but also prescribe and justify forms of global advocacy. Historical developments lend force to Beitz's observation that "to whatever extent contemporary international political life can be said to have a 'sense of justice,' its language is the language of human rights."[5] Human rights advocates, as agents of justice, have helped to create that language. Seen in this way, the creation of practical tools for justice-seeking should be considered a signal achievement of the international human rights movement.

We can learn about the process of justice-seeking from the contents of regular, public, and transnational claims launched by non-governmental actors on behalf of the human rights of individuals. Amnesty International was a pioneer in this form of public action for global human rights. The activism it engendered first sought to protect people from physical harm by governments and to protest the denial of civil and political rights. Amnesty International aspired for its approach to be universal in theme and applicability, but appeals were launched with reference to very specific circumstances of political repression of named individuals and groups. Its techniques have been imitated, supplemented, complemented, and, it is possible, may one day be supplanted by the work of fellow NGOs of many shapes and sizes. However, the approaches AI created and popularized, which I focus on as exemplars in Chapters 4 and 5, have been long-lasting and adaptable. They constitute a unique kind of action for global justice that integrates active care with politics and law.

There is a significant aspect of justice related to human rights that AI and its leading globally focused counterparts, including Human Rights Watch, recognized but did not initially incorporate in their active rights work. Even though the Universal Declaration of Human Rights (UDHR) translates basic features of economic, social, and

---

[5] Charles Beitz, "Human Rights as a Common Concern," *American Political Science Review* 95, no. 2 (2001): 269.

cultural equity and well-being into the language of economic, social, and cultural (ESC) rights, it has taken a long time for large NGOs to begin to address social justice issues. In another sector entirely, Oxfam, the anti-poverty NGO, turned to rights to complement its own advocacy on global economic and social issues. Oxfam adopted a "basic rights" approach to its development work in the 1990s, as did a large number of other development NGOs. Now, AI and Human Rights Watch not only include statements about social justice in their programming but also defend individuals who are engaged at the local level in claiming social, economic, and cultural rights. Contemporary human rights advocates have begun to apply human rights language, and human rights demands, to new social justice issues, suggesting a possible convergence over time on human rights as a language of justice.

Justice has also made its own demands of human rights advocacy. Until the 1990s, many activists in the Global North tended to see *themselves* as "lifting up the issues," as one longtime human rights professional reflected critically.[6] The 1990s marked the initiation of much richer exchange between activists in the Global North and the Global South, as I describe in Chapter 6.[7] To this day, domestic movements and global activists continue to identify challenges to justice as they occur within NGOs' own networks. Because of the demands of justice, nearly all NGOs are working to address gender, race, diversity,

---

[6] Ellen Dorsey, interviewed by Ann Marie Clark, telephone, July 2, 2018.

[7] The terms "Global North" and "Global South" are widely used to refer to developed and developing countries, respectively. The usage is traceable to a 1980 report on global development, known as the Brandt Commission report. See "The North–South Divide," in Independent Commission on International Development Issues, *North–South, a Programme for Survival: Report of the Independent Commission on International Development Issues* (Cambridge, MA: MIT Press, 1980), 31. For a more accurate geographical picture of development, see Royal Geographical Society, *The Global North/South Divide* (London: Royal Geographical Society). www.rgs.org/CM SPages/GetFile.aspx?nodeguid=9c1ce781-9117-4741-af0a-a6a8b75f32b4&lang=en-GB.

and equity concerns within their own networks as well as out in the world.

Justice Ideas and Human Rights

The practice of human rights at the global level supports several important aspects of justice, including the conduct of law, equality, freedom of the individual, and security of the person. Debates about the relative priority of aspects of justice infuse philosophical questions about how to recognize the absence of justice, how justice should be constructed if we were building social institutions from scratch, and how to achieve more justice starting from current circumstances. As a set of principles and practices, human rights have the most to contribute to the first and last question: How to recognize injustice, and what can be done to get more justice? This section explores conceptions of justice and the implications of human rights for justice in global politics.

The relevance of human rights to justice in the world, and the place human rights occupies in a contemporary sense of justice, has thus far been treated more thoroughly by political theorists and philosophers than by social scientists who study causal propositions about human rights action in international politics. Here I offer a very brief survey of ideas in the justice literature pertinent to human rights. To situate my examination of human rights through a justice lens, I draw propositions about components of action for justice from theoretical discussions of human rights and justice, and link them with empirical research on recent patterns of human rights action in global politics. This enables me to build a theoretically grounded account of human rights as an observable and incremental justice practice.

Thinking about human rights mirrors the divide between ideal and nonideal understandings of justice. Ideal theories of justice, as Michael Goodhart explains, "aim to establish what justice is and requires in its pure form."[8] In other words, an ideal theory seeks to define principles of justice as a comprehensive set of institutional arrangements for a just society. The logic of universal human rights, as a set of principles outlining how individual societies should be organized, is compatible with ideal theory. For example, the human rights principles presented in the UDHR,[9] and the related treaties that further articulate human rights, are clear statements of standards for how governments should treat people.

Because human rights principles are now widely recognized internationally, it is common for theoretical treatments of justice and of human rights to characterize human rights principles as something most people, in the abstract, could agree on when considering desirable political institutions. Nation-states, in fact, agreed to that list of human rights in 1948. John Rawls, author of one of the best-known ideal theories of justice, derived criteria for fairness in society based on whether one would choose them in advance as institutional arrangements without knowing one's own place in society.[10] Rawls later stipulated human rights principles as shorthand for a number of institutional requirements for a well-ordered society.[11]

The view of human rights as a version of justice principles appears elsewhere in the political theory literature. Jack Donnelly, for example, writes that broad social consensus about the content of human rights qualifies human rights as a "political conception of

---

[8] Michael E. Goodhart, *Injustice: Political Theory for the Real World* (Oxford: Oxford University Press, 2018), 25.

[9] "Universal Declaration of Human Rights" (U.N.G.A. res. 217A (III), U.N. Doc A/810 at 71, December 8, 1948).

[10] John Rawls, *A Theory of Justice* (Cambridge, MA: Belknap Press of Harvard University Press, 1971).

[11] John Rawls, *The Law of Peoples* (Cambridge, MA: Harvard University Press, 1999), 36.

justice."[12] The theorized consensus over human rights as the basis for a set of just institutional rules makes it relatively uncontroversial to stipulate human rights principles as political principles of justice.

Further, the proposition that human rights are available as stand-ins for ideal political arrangements moves beyond the idea that human rights are simply moral notions of what is due to individuals as members of humanity, as Laura Valentini notes.[13] In defining how one evaluates the justice of political institutions, human rights "seem essentially to function as standards of global justice."[14] But Valentini cautions that, if rights are to matter as political standards of justice, they should do more than structure institutions. Human rights as standards of justice should also actively protect people's most important interests from encroachment by "inescapable" global institutions, such as "states, some powerful institutions, and the practices of international finance and trade."[15]

Human Rights as Tools for Justice Rather Than a Measure of Justice

The ability to frame justice concerns as human rights today stems from the broad political and social acceptance of the ideals that human rights embody. Rather than use human rights as a proxy for justice, however,

---

[12] Jack Donnelly, "Human Rights," in *The Oxford Handbook of Political Theory*, eds. John S. Dryzek, Bonnie Honig, and Anne Phillips (Oxford: Oxford University Press, 2006), 40. Donnelly characterizes the conception as the "UDHR model"; Beitz refers to the use of rights as a plausible representation of consensus about moral expectations as the "agreement model" in *The Idea of Human Rights*, 73. It should also be noted that although many of its principles are far-sighted, the UDHR also reflects its temporal context, so that as a practical political conception of justice, the UDHR would need to be updated.

[13] Laura Valentini, "In What Sense Are Human Rights Political? A Preliminary Exploration," *Political Studies* 60 (2012): 180–194.

[14] Ibid., 184. [15] Ibid., 184.

my approach will be to investigate, rather than elide, the distinction between human rights and justice. Human rights are now globally accepted norms. The UDHR, which enumerates a broad set of civil, political, economic, and cultural rights, is complemented by an array of global and regional treaties and other standards, as well as national laws. Beitz makes the case that human rights have begun to be constitutive of global institutions and as such have begun to change the conditions for the pursuit of justice politics globally.[16] Human rights are embedded, institutionally and legally, in world politics. In this respect, they comprise a common point of reference for a shared sense of justice.

Beitz is not the only theorist to refer to a sense of justice as the ability and seemingly widely shared motivation people have to consider, evaluate, and implement just and fair treatment. David Johnston describes the human capacity for a sense of justice as "the capacity to engage in evaluations about matters of justice and fairness and to be moved by judgments about such matters."[17] He traces the sense of justice in philosophy to Aristotle's discussion of the human capacity for language and categorization, which enables us to make and share judgments and comparisons. When I refer to a sense of justice in the chapters that follow, I do so with Johnston's account in mind. In explicit and implicit ways, a sense of justice can shape whether and how people choose to act either together or individually in response to perceived injustice.

As Goodhart notes, people involved in human rights advocacy rarely "imagine that they are working to build a perfectly just society

---

[16] On the importance of institutions to rights, in addition to Beitz, *The Idea of Human Rights*, see also Charles R. Beitz and Robert E. Goodin, *Global Basic Rights* (Oxford: Oxford University Press, 2009). Of particular interest in this volume, dedicated to the work of Henry Shue, are the introductory chapter by the editors, "Introduction: Basic Rights and Beyond," 1–24; and Christian Reus-Smit, "On Rights and Institutions," 25–48.

[17] David Johnston, *A Brief History of Justice* (Chichester: Wiley-Blackwell, 2011), 13.

from the ground up, or that the rights they advocate reflect timeless philosophical truths ... They view human rights as tools for challenging unjust laws, norms and institutions."[18] In Goodhart's view, human rights do not portend an ideal form of justice, even if some philosophers may refer to them as versions of just social arrangements. Instead, human rights in politics are better understood as "a dynamic response to people's actual experiences of oppression."[19]

Human rights norms can thus be viewed as furnishing a way of interpreting political and social wrongs in a changing international system. The departing point for my analysis is a view of human rights practice as an empirical field for observing how new resources of justice – discourse and action appealing to principles of justice – emerge historically, often in response to changes in actors' sense of what justice calls for. If a sense of justice emerges through evaluations and judgments of human agents, it may also be refined through experience. A critical view suggests that increasingly diverse participants in a global dialogue about justice can also be expected to challenge and change conceptions of what justice demands.

The language of justice is dynamic, just as the sense of justice has been historically dynamic, meaning that it is subject to change. For example, in the words of AI's founder Peter Benenson in 1961, AI's work was about remembering "the forgotten prisoner."[20] Looking back, that phrase may be read as extending a one-sided kind of patronage. In a dynamic conception of this "remembering" activity initiated by Benenson and colleagues, however, one can observe that ten years later, AI staff and volunteers were building information conduits and action plans that flowed back and forth between activists and people

---

[18] Goodhart, *Injustice: Political Theory for the Real World*, 101.

[19] Ibid., 144. Goodhart reminds us that human rights are best understood in light of a politics of justice, not an ideal understanding of justice, so that the rights necessary for human emancipation "cannot be a fixed list" (ibid.).

[20] Peter Benenson, "The Forgotten Prisoners," *The Observer*, May 28, 1961, 21.

under threat. This exchange of information was unusual for that time and predates Margaret Keck and Kathryn Sikkink's time line for the emergence of fully fledged transnational human rights advocacy networks.[21] The extended, repeated contact that AI researchers and volunteers initiated with advocates on the ground in repressive countries was already transforming the conscience of advocates, leading them to change their practices of advocacy, and the relevant sense of justice, even in the very early period.

Political movements for justice, even in established democracies, use human rights language to express the gravity of contemporaneous justice concerns. Just as rights should be understood dynamically, according to Goodhart, the understanding of injustice itself must also be "dynamic and provisional."[22] People alter applications of rights in response to their political and social circumstances.[23] As we know from a number of studies, activists turn human rights language into the vernacular and use it to seek justice in contexts that were not necessarily envisioned in 1948.[24] Rights have become "popular": so popular that "the language of human rights is a political claim-making discourse for judging governments and corporate actors."[25] Moreover, social movements often use rights language in new,

---

[21] Margaret Keck and Kathryn Sikkink, *Activists beyond Borders* (Ithaca, NY: Cornell University Press, 1998).

[22] Goodhart, *Injustice: Political Theory for the Real World*, 144.

[23] See, for example, Jackie Smith, "Domesticating International Human Rights Norms," in *Social Movements for Global Democracy* (Baltimore: Johns Hopkins University Press, 2008), 158–176.

[24] Shareen Hertel, *Unexpected Power: Conflict and Change among Transnational Activists* (Ithaca, NY: Cornell University Press, 2006); Sally Engle Merry, *Human Rights and Gender Violence: Translating International Law into Local Justice* (Chicago: University of Chicago Press, 2006).

[25] Geoff Dancy and Christopher Fariss, "The Heavens Are Always Fallen: A Neo-constitutive Approach to Human Rights in Global Society," *Law and Contemporary Problems* 81, no. 4 (2018): 86.

nonstandard ways that challenge earlier conceptions of the proper content of rights. Human rights language and practices accepted as standard now were once new as well.

Laura Valentini refers to an incremental approach to justice as "transitional," conceiving the objective as making the world more just from the present forward, rather than conceiving an ideal end-state.[26] Practical action on human rights faces up against injustice.[27] Because human rights actors work in the world as it is, but with a vision of what it can be, a nonideal understanding of justice facilitates a more fruitful consideration of the facets of justice encompassed in human rights practice.

Conclusion

I will appeal to dynamic and incremental views of justice to establish a conception of human rights practice as an array of tools of justice. For this, we need to work with nonideal theory, attempting to build a theoretical understanding of what is required to move closer to a just world. Here, theoretical thinking about human rights as moving incrementally toward more fully realized justice is most helpful. If, instead of making human rights a proxy for a justice ideal, we switch that logic to emphasize human rights work as a set of repeated attempts to introduce justice concerns into politics, the focal point shifts away from the ideal and toward practical action. It becomes possible to theorize about the significance, for justice, of changes in human rights practices over time.

Human rights advocacy has built a series of tools for the pursuit of justice. It has expanded the scope of human concern in the global neighborhood. It has created a distinct language of globally recognized

---

[26] Laura Valentini, "Ideal vs. Non-ideal Theory: A Conceptual Map," *Philosophy Compass* 7, no. 9 (2012): 654–664. See also Amartya Sen's discussion in *The Idea of Justice* (Cambridge, MA: Belknap Press of Harvard University Press, 2009); as well as Goodhart's extended discussion in *Injustice: Political Theory for the Real World*.

[27] Goodhart, *Injustice: Political Theory for the Real World*.

appeals, within which law and concern can be expressed as demands for just treatment of persons. The language has been taken up by other actors, including economic development advocates like Oxfam, to reinforce the political agency of people who suffer from social injustice. In the next chapter, I introduce each component of justice more systematically and illustrate it through research on the associated cases in later chapters to observe each set of justice dynamics through archival material, interviews, and secondary accounts. Table 2.1 summarizes the justice components, associated human rights tools, and the observable implications explored in the chapters that follow.

Table 2.1 *Components of global justice, related human rights tools, and observable implications*

	Features	Human rights tools	Observable implications (evidence)
Justice of neighborhood	Common concern; broadening the scope of concern; focus on the impact of rights violations on individual lives; emergency response	Active care; habit; appeals as expressions of transnational concern	Transnational expressions of concern for individuals affected by human rights violations, e.g., the Urgent Action alerts of AI
Political realization of justice	Norms constructed and embedded in a structure of law and legal remedy; creation of institutions; legal guarantees providing for freedom and civil justice	Law as a formal structure of human rights standards; emergence of a human rights culture of argument invoking law as a political tool, in addition to care	Development of human rights law; incorporation of law into human rights appeals

Table 2.1 (cont.)

	Features	Human rights tools	Observable implications (evidence)
Integrated social justice	Economic and distributive equality; global solidarity; respect for ESC rights	Human rights to recognize and represent the agency of those affected; assertion of ESC rights; domestic "translations" of global rights into vernacular contexts	Application of human rights language to ESC issues; use of human rights by economic justice groups (e.g., Oxfam) to address structural injustice; global protection of human rights defenders who work on a wider range of issues than traditional civil and political rights conceptions

What does the early work tell us about the basic tools of advocacy for underrepresented causes? To specify the tools of human rights from separate justice-related vantage points requires tacking back and forth between the concrete and theoretical. On the concrete side, it is important to identify what specific tools of action the human rights movement has introduced to global politics, and to describe their emergence in the late twentieth century. On the abstract side, such tools have not yet been situated in the context of a theory and politics of justice. I make a beginning here.

3

Human Rights Tools in the Pursuit of Justice

Human rights protection efforts have modeled new approaches to global justice that also draw strength from old, neighborly impulses to reduce the suffering of distant individuals. From the early days of global humanitarian action, people have organized ways to provide material aid in far-away places in cases of emergency, often in areas where local governments have limited capacity for response or are simply over-whelmed by disaster.[1] The human rights movement, however, made new forms of action possible by activists on behalf of distant individuals under acute or imminent threat from their own governments and related political, economic, and social forces. At the end of Chapter 2, I introduced a shorthand for three components of justice that have been introduced into global politics through human rights practice: neighborhood; political realization of justice; and the integration of social justice. In this chapter, I discuss the tools that human rights advocates have developed to put these components of justice into practice.

The Justice of Neighborhood

The concept of neighborhood is helpful as a way of referring to relatively loose ties that may be activated contingently in response to need at the global level. Amartya Sen uses the biblical Good Samaritan story to inform a conception of relations in a global neighborhood.[2] The

---

[1] David P. Forsythe, *The Humanitarians: The International Committee of the Red Cross* (New York: Cambridge University Press, 2005); Michael Barnett, *Empire of Humanity: A History of Humanitarianism* (Ithaca, NY: Cornell University Press, 2011).

[2] Sen, *The Idea of Justice*, 170–173.

Good Samaritan parable is well known, but I summarize it here because, for Sen, it is a metaphor for understanding conditions conducive to action for global justice. I use Sen's discussion to frame how human rights practice develops an expanded circle of concern for others as part of getting to justice. I refer to this as the "justice of neighborhood."

In response to the command to love one's neighbor, a lawyer asks Jesus of Nazareth, "Who is my neighbor?"[3] Jesus responds with the story of a man stripped, robbed, beaten, and left for dead at the side of a road outside of the city of Jerusalem. After two separate passersby, respected community members, have crossed the road to avoid the wounded man, a traveler from Samaria stops to help. The Samaritan "bandaged his wounds, ... brought him to an inn, and took care of him." In the biblical context, the audience would likely have viewed Samaritans as outsiders of lesser status, certainly not legitimate "neighbors," but Jesus puts the question back to the lawyer: Who was his neighbor? The lawyer, having tried to elicit narrow and specific rules of obligation, admits that the neighbor was "the one who showed him mercy." The underlying implication is that the neighbor was not defined by proximity, identity, or some other rule, but by his actions.

Sen reads the parable as a "rejection of the idea of a fixed neighbourhood."[4] He ties this story directly to a central premise of global justice as resting on "our relations with distant people."[5] The justice of neighborhood also rejects the idea that global justice should be defined as relations among states. Even many justice theorists adopt a statist framework that sees justice in international politics as a matter

[3] Biblical quotations are from "Luke 10:25–35: Parable of the Good Samaritan," in *Holy Bible, New Revised Standard Version* (New York: American Bible Society, 1989).

[4] Sen, *The Idea of Justice*, 171.

[5] Ibid., 172. Here, Sen argues against John Rawls and other theorists who limit consideration of just institutional arrangements to what pertains within national boundaries.

of relations within and among nation-states. Rarely is justice formulated as action for distant individuals in a global context.

I draw on Sen's discussion to conceive of a justice of neighborhood related to human rights. A justice of neighborhood incorporates neighborly responsibilities. A justice of neighborhood is clearly not fully adequate for achieving global justice because nation-states and global economic structures are implicated in global injustices. Some forms of care introduced by human rights practices are characteristic of the justice of neighborhood, however. Human rights help people to recognize the situations of individuals suffering injustice, and enable ordinary individuals to express support for distant persons whose human rights are at risk.

Beyond that vision, human rights advocates have developed practices – contingent and experimental at first – that offer concrete actions one can take on the way to recognizing and protecting the personhood of the global neighbor. Some actions, like small acts of assistance people share with neighbors, do not necessarily require great investment in order to expand the boundaries of the neighborhood. The justice of neighborhood envisioned in human rights practices is based on extending forms of aid and protection to persons in emergency situations and in situations of threat. This facet of justice positions human rights violations in other places as something to care about and supplies repertoires of action aimed at directly helping others in need, reminding us of the value of the material and incremental aspects of human rights work.

The Tools of Justice of Neighborhood: Active Care, Habit, and Appeals

The human rights movement employs three tools characteristic of the justice of neighborhood: care, habit, and appeals. Active care in the human rights context is best exemplified by intervention mobilized in response to need, especially in emergency. Active care becomes a part of justice through habit and repetition. A habit of ongoing, active care – unceasing work to collect information and coordinate action – transforms and uplifts the neighborhood. Appeals to authority on behalf of others are the principal human rights tool linking the justice of neighborhood to politics. I discuss each of these in turn.

Active Care

The work of human rights as a neighborly response to emergency is frequently oriented toward the abatement of harm, and brings with it both the benefits of palliation and the limitations. For the individuals affected, the extension of care can mean alleviation of suffering, healing, and even survival. However, palliative work is undertaken, often, within unjust political, economic, and social structures.

That is why I emphasize the importance of active care as a tool of the justice of neighborhood. Active care accords the neighbor equal respect and value when attempting to alleviate suffering, human need, and threat. It anticipates a mutual relationship of equality so that assistance, from the giver's perspective, must be checked for errors of imagination and self-reference. With regard to justice, a misplaced sense of identification or pity has been recognized as problematic by critics of "welfarist" development practices because such dispositions may do little to address inequality and may reinforce subordination.[6]

Active care shares some features with compassion. Compassion itself is not an action, but it can prompt a desire to act. Scholarly studies of human rights have not fully appreciated the importance of compassion, according to Rhoda Howard-Hassmann:

> Human beings . . . can imagine what it is like to live in circumstances not their own. They can also make moral choices about their own

[6] Jennifer Rubenstein, *Between Samaritans and States: The Political Ethics of Humanitarian NGOs* (Oxford: Oxford University Press, 2015).

obligations to even the most distant of others. Members of human rights organizations – including those from the most privileged social backgrounds – often make huge sacrifices and frequently risk their lives to assist others.[7]

Active care as a tool of justice has two aspects: care as taking an interest or concern, and care as the action of caring for persons. The justice of neighborhood requires both kinds of care to work together. The first aspect of care, taking an interest, calls for adapting one's neighborliness to what one's neighbors actually require. Concern that is supported by thinking and openness to a change in understanding is part of active care. If that openness to new understanding is missing, care is potentially distorted in a way that does not fully respect human rights.

Care's second aspect entails being prepared to take action. A point I will return to is the centrality of emergency care in the justice of neighborhood. Emergency care depends on swift action, facilitated by preparation. In an emergency as an individual caregiver might experience it, the action of caring may be spontaneous, as the Samaritan's was. He cared for the injured man when faced with immediate need. This logic captures the contingency of emergency response that can initiate a sense of neighborhood out of the action of caring. The action of caring does not become a practice of the justice of neighborhood, however, until it is also informed by care in the sense of taking an interest – learning how to care – and preparing oneself to care more actively.

Active care in the human rights realm is enabled by human rights advocates' provision of information and methods for engaging in transnational action on behalf of individuals' human rights. The human rights movement builds the global neighborhood by enlarging the

---

[7] Rhoda Howard-Hassmann, *In Defense of Universal Human Rights* (Cambridge: Polity Press, 2019), 37.

bounds of the neighborhood and enlisting interested new neighborhood members as participants in acts of caring. Not all human rights organizations invite the kind of direct participation that was an early hallmark of Amnesty International (AI), but they all offer forms of direct or indirect participation in a politics informed by concerns characteristic of the justice of neighborhood. Some do so through direct support and appeals, others involve the public in lobbying and other forms of campaigning on human rights issues. Other indirect actions of care include collaboration among local, regional, and global advocates. Global women's human rights activists have worked especially hard, and have been especially successful, at these kinds of linkages. In the relation between global and local, caring "about" the neighbor carries a responsibility for adaptation. Brooke Ackerly has coined the term, "connected activists," an apt phrasing for agents of human rights work who use both expertise and connection to further the cause of justice.[8]

In addition, the activation of care can prompt difficult negotiations and even conflict within networks. Human rights organizations and transnational activist networks of other kinds still grapple with internal justice of global connections among activists working in differing contexts. Differences in power, strategy, and in the structure of relations among organizational networks are common.[9] North–South variation in human rights groups' objectives for human rights activism also characterizes the global neighborhood.[10]

---

[8] Brooke A. Ackerly, *Just Responsibility: A Human Rights Theory of Global Justice* (Oxford: Oxford University Press, 2018).

[9] For example, see Wendy H. Wong, *Internal Affairs: How the Structure of NGOs Transforms Human Rights* (Ithaca, NY: Cornell University Press, 2012); R. Charli Carpenter, *Lost Causes: Agenda Vetting in Global Issue Networks and the Shaping of Human Security* (Ithaca, NY: Cornell University Press, 2016); Hertel, *Unexpected Power*; Sarah S. Stroup and Wendy H. Wong, *The Authority Trap: Strategic Choices of International NGOs* (Ithaca, NY: Cornell University Press, 2017).

[10] See for example, Sarah S. Stroup and Amanda Murdie, "There's No Place Like Home: Explaining International NGO Advocacy," *The Review of International*

Habits of Daily Work

Just as care is the first tool that informs human rights responses to information about urgent need, habit is a second, underestimated tool that extends such care by preparing for emergencies in the neighborhood, allowing people to be better neighbors. Habits of action are visible almost everywhere people are making extra efforts for justice. The skills honed by habit support advocates' readiness to act.

For a person who is a human rights advocate, whether a professional or volunteer, action that makes up the justice of neighborhood is repetitive and difficult. There are always new cases, new people, new situations – requiring constant attention to persons experiencing risk, threat, and harm. There may be little immediate reward compared with the demands required to respond repeatedly to the same patterns of violation. Although it may be obvious that structural remedies would be better in the long term, the justice of neighborhood responds to suffering in the here and now.

An ongoing readiness of habit has been observed in individuals who come to the aid of others. Moreover, a habit of care appears to be reinforced by the expression of care. According to Kristina Thalhammer and her coauthors, "Holocaust rescuers in general were ordinary people who habitually cared about and for others."[11] When people recognize injustice and act, however, they may be

> permanently transformed by what they have done. Further, they often
> transform the context by providing an example or reinterpretation of

Organizations 7, no. 4 (2012): 425–448. See also Ann Marie Clark, Elisabeth J. Friedman, and Kathryn Hochstetler, "The Sovereign Limits of Global Civil Society: A Comparison of NGO Participation in UN World Conferences on the Environment, Human Rights, and Women," *World Politics* 51, no. 1 (1998): 1–35.

[11] Kristina E. Thalhammer, Paula O'Laughlin, Myron Peretz Glazer, et al., *Courageous Resistance: The Power of Ordinary People* (New York: Palgrave Macmillan, 2007), 23; citing Samuel P. Oliner and Pearl M. Oliner, *The Altruistic Personality: Rescuers of Jews in Nazi Europe* (New York: Free Press, 1988).

events for [other] potential courageous resisters and often leave a legacy of networks or institutional change resulting from their actions.[12]

Similarly, Daniel Carpenter and Colin Moore have found that involvement in petitioning, a less risky form of political organizing and persuasion, has legacy effects on individuals' later propensity to engage in advocacy for causes that they care about.[13] The habits of human rights response fostered by nongovernmental human rights organizations have formed a collective legacy, making it possible for like-minded individuals to participate in habits of resistance to injustice.

Repeated intervention in situations of political emergencies is a form of daily toil, a phrase that Bonnie Honig has used in a different context with reference to the slow, regular work needed to keep democracy vital.[14] Such work takes time, and operates in steady counterpoint to the frantic pace of emergency. Honig's discussion informs my understanding of habit as a tool for the justice of neighborhood because much of the work of human rights advocates is characterized by ongoing efforts to close the gap between the promise of human rights and the reality of human rights abuses. Repeated work in the face of this gap paves a way for people to begin to recover justice in situations of emergency. The work entailed in organizing and maintaining AI's Urgent Action (UA) network, described in Chapter 4, demonstrates readiness to act that is supported by the repetitive effort needed to maintain a safety net for individuals in danger globally.

---

[12] Thalhammer et al., *Courageous Resistance*, 37.

[13] Daniel Carpenter and Colin D. Moore, "When Canvassers Became Activists: Antislavery Petitioning and the Political Mobilization of American Women," *American Political Science Review* 108, no. 3 (2014): 479–498.

[14] Bonnie Honig, *Emergency Politics: Paradox, Law, Democracy* (Princeton, NJ: Princeton University Press, 2009).

The shortcomings of emergency care invite a discussion not only of its limitations but also of the differential power held by actors in the global neighborhood, and thus of the limitations posed by political structures in the global system. Nongovernmental organizations' (NGOs') capacities to act, as Jennifer Rubenstein recognizes, usually cannot match that of governments. NGOs are second-best for responding to crises, partly because of capacity, but also because NGOs do not carry the same responsibility for democratic representation that governments do. Governments ought to be, and often are, better at responding either jointly or individually, to resource and security emergencies.[15] However, one of the paradoxes of human rights politics is that in human rights emergencies, government agents – or people or organizations acting with the acquiescence of ruling authorities – are commonly the culprits. In addition, states' capacities vary. As Onora O'Neill recognizes, international NGOs and other non-state actors qualify only as "secondary" agents of justice because states generally possess greater capability and bear more direct duties. International NGOs' advocacy for justice still matters, especially because

> [o]nce we look at the realities of life where states are weak, any simple division between primary and secondary agents of justice blurs. Justice has to be built by a diversity of agents and agencies that possess and lack varying ranges of capabilities, and that can contribute to justice – or to injustice – in more diverse ways than is generally acknowledged.[16]

As I have discussed in this section, NGOs' repertoires of response are foundational to their contributions to justice. This does not mean that they are sufficient. It should also be pointed out that some scholars have developed extensive critiques of the human rights

---

[15] Rubenstein, *Between Samaritans and States.*

[16] Onora O'Neill, "Agents of Justice," *Metaphilosophy* 32, no. 1/2 (2001): 194.

regime from race, gender, and postcolonial perspectives. Such critiques call for more transformational politics than might be associated with the tools of neighborhood, and even for transformed human rights conceptions.[17] The tools of neighborhood are often palliative in the moment, but as I argue in discussing human rights appeals, they can also be used to articulate the need for justice.

Appeals

The appeal is a third tool rooted in the justice of neighborhood. The appeal is the most political tool of the three because it gives voice to the less powerful and, as used by the human rights community, makes demands of those in power. To appeal is to make an "earnest request" of another for help, or for a decision of some import that may impact either oneself or a third party.[18] Amnesty International's appeals have historically focused on named individuals and small groups, in a case-by-case approach that catalogs potential human rights violations while at the same time demanding redress for the individual. Many other organizations and individuals have used forms of appeal for human rights and for other justice causes.

Some appeals in the broader human rights neighborhood demonstrate creative, even symbolic, calls for new forms of justice. Appeals may dramatize, express, stake a claim, or negotiate. They may be literal or symbolic. Appeals made by different actors for the

---

[17] See, for example, Julia Suárez-Krabbe, "The Other Side of the Story: Human Rights, Race and Gender from a Transatlantic Perspective," in *Decolonizing Enlightenment: Transnational Justice, Human Rights and Democracy in a Postcolonial World*, ed. Nikita Dhawan, 211–226 (Opladen: Barbara Budrich, 2014); Julia Suárez-Krabbe, "Race, Social Struggles and 'Human' Rights: Contributions from the Global South," in *Europe and the Americas: Transatlantic Approaches to Human Rights*, eds. Erik André Andersen and Eva Maria Lassen, 41–52 (Leiden: Brill Nijhoff, 2015).

[18] "Appeal," in *The Concise Oxford Dictionary*, ed. J. B. Sykes (Oxford: Oxford University Press, 1982).

same cause may draw attention to different aspects of a situation and can vary widely in their content and context.

The strategies and styles of appeal can vary among political actors on the same side of an issue. In the years after Augusto Pinochet took power in Chile in 1973, activist lawyers regularly lodged conventional appeals for *amparo* (i.e., *habeas corpus*) on behalf of each known disappeared person. The appeals for *amparo* used the legal procedure not only to pursue procedural justice but to put the cases on record in the absence of justice, and to share with sources outside of Chile.[19] In Argentina, mothers and grandmothers of the Disappeared called publicly and repeatedly for investigation and accountability for those responsible for the disappearances of their relatives in the Argentine "Dirty War" of the late 1970s and early 1980s. Some of the mothers of the Disappeared radically broke from the appeals of other Argentine human rights groups when they adopted the slogan, "*aparición con vida*": appearance of their disappeared relatives "with life."[20] Members of the Argentine human rights movement debated how and whether to even use the word justice, as Kathryn Sikkink recounts. By 1983, according to Sikkink, the human rights movement in Argentina was demanding not only justice but "*juicio y castigo*" (trials and punishment) for human rights violations, and Argentina became one of the first countries to prosecute human rights violators.[21]

---

[19] On Chile, see Ann Marie Clark, *Diplomacy of Conscience: Amnesty International and Changing International Human Rights Norms* (Princeton, NJ: Princeton University Press, 2001), 78–79.

[20] Berber Bevernage, *History, Memory, and State-Sponsored Violence: Time and Justice* (New York: Routledge, 2012), 39. Rosa Linda Fregoso describes a more recent slogan, "*Las queremos vivas*" ("We want them alive"), used in Mexico to protest women's deaths, recalling the language of Argentina's *Madres* as "a demand for justice and state accountability." See Fregoso, "'We Want Them Alive!': The Politics and Culture of Human Rights," *Social Identities* 12, no. 2 (2006): 127.

[21] Kathryn Sikkink, *The Justice Cascade: How Human Rights Prosecutions Are Changing World Politics* (New York: W. W. Norton, 2011), 67–70.

In making a concrete demand – as justice appeals regularly do – an appeal may refer both to what is ideal and what is possible to achieve. Lea Ypi argues that political action for justice requires this combination.[22] The demand of *aparición con vida* asks for what may be impossible. Even the contemporaneous *amparo* filings in Chile, demanding information as to the whereabouts of the Disappeared, were bold and, undoubtedly, unrealistic requests in the midst of brutal repression. Initial calls for trials in Argentina were considered naïve, but within a few years, "Argentines in the human rights movement had moved from fear of putting the word 'justice' in their slogans to ... referring to trials and to punishment."[23]

Appeals are discursive acts intended to have practical implications, making them useful tools for human rights advocates in the absence of material power or other relevant resources. In the case of large and complicated global problems, discussion needs to reach many audiences. Just as human rights advocates have debated what kinds of words and actions are appropriate for their goals, not all audiences view a problem in the same way or see the same arguments as relevant. O'Neill argued in a 1986 essay on the nuclear weapons debate that advocates should appeal to others with arguments that are accessible and "action-guiding" for their target audiences.[24] The hoped-for response may not be forthcoming, but "even if ethical reasoning can gain no purchase in the world as it is, it may be possible to change the world into one where it is accessible for some relevant agents."[25] In other words, appeals addressing hearers in the present may also build

---

[22] Lea Ypi, *Global Justice and Avant-Garde Political Agency* (Oxford: Oxford University Press, 2012).

[23] Sikkink, *The Justice Cascade*, 68–69.

[24] Onora O'Neill, "Who Can Endeavour Peace?," *Canadian Journal of Philosophy* 16, no. supp. 1 (1986): 46.

[25] Ibid., 68.

conditions for later reasoning about action. Both are significant features of appeals as I theorize them in the human rights context.

This section has suggested that human rights movement practices have cultivated an ethical shift that supports direct responses to injustice, and that this shift was central to a justice of neighborhood. What frustrated the lawyer in the story of the Good Samaritan is that the enactment of a justice of neighborhood is not based on a systematic account of rights and obligations. He wanted to know the limits of his duties, but as the lawyer seemed to recognize, the question of limits is not answered within a justice of neighborhood. Instead, human rights practices that build the justice of neighborhood depend on regular expression of concern – frequently directed at political authorities, but not necessarily on political terms – for persons whose lives and well-being are actively threatened.

Human rights appeals load the choice of action with great urgency, even though appeals may focus on harms that are distant from those whose participation they seek to enlist. The urgency is intensified by the hope of preventing or mitigating the harm to individuals when rights are under threat. As a tool of the justice of neighborhood, appeals proclaim the extension of the neighborhood as they make justice demands that may place political demands on power-holders and on fellow neighbors. The appeal therefore has the potential to link the justice of neighborhood with steps toward the realization of justice in politics, which is a focus of the next section.

In Chapter 4, the tools of care, habit, and appeal are illustrated through the story of how the UA technique was invented by AI's headquarters in London and how staffers and volunteers developed distribution networks for the UA alerts in the USA and Germany. Amnesty International had initiated a famous approach to human rights appeals, beginning with a newspaper appeal in 1961, which was transformed into an ongoing campaign through the formation of local member groups in numerous countries.[26] Group members took on a few prisoners' cases at a time, from a selection of political systems, in order to press for their release via letter and telegram in the name of freedom of conscience. The UA technique is less well known. Invented by AI staffers in 1971, Urgent Action also relied on written correspondence but produced faster, more targeted appeals for people under threat in a wider range of circumstances. Urgent Action proved to be a simple and durable approach to appeals, and has been widely copied by other organizations. The story of the UA technique is fascinating not just as a stand-alone narrative of how a lasting approach to advocacy developed but also as an illustration of how practitioners became aware that new techniques were needed to move closer to justice.

The Political Realization of Justice

By turning to law and global legal norms to support human rights in the realm of international politics, human rights advocates positioned human rights as a more explicitly political realization of justice. The political realization of justice refers to efforts to fulfill justice by establishing political tools for its accomplishment. Political and legal advocacy for human rights cases has built a new global human rights discourse, which I refer to as a human rights culture of argument. The human rights culture of argument unites two facets of justice: the

---

[26] Tom Buchanan, "'The Truth Will Set You Free': The Making of Amnesty International," *Journal of Contemporary History* 37, no. 4 (2002): 575–597. Buchanan demystifies and contextualizes some of the lore of AI's founding, noting that the idea of an "appeal for amnesty" had already been used on behalf of communists imprisoned in Spain, Portugal, and Greece (but not by AI's founders). Amnesty International's contribution, according to Buchanan, was to move away from partisanship for whatever "cause" prisoners might advocate, and defend their freedom of speech (ibid., 579–580).

care of neighborhood and the political realization of justice through rights and law.

Tools of the Political Realization of Justice: Law and a Human Rights Culture of Argument

The political realization of justice requires tools beyond those of the justice of neighborhood. The first, prominent in international human rights practice, is law. The articulation of legal norms related to human rights has permitted human rights advocates to invoke law as a generalized response to urgency. The second tool made possible by uniting legal arguments with the justice of neighborhood is a human rights culture of argument, a way of arguing for justice that is rooted in human rights. This discourse has become a way for people to talk about a broad scope of justice concerns as they participate in politics.

As political science scholarship and the field reporting by major NGOs demonstrates, human rights abuses are symptomatic of political threats as well as humanitarian threats. Characteristic patterns of human rights abuses may be driven not only by objective conditions of emergency but by ideological and political rationales that define certain people or groups as the targets of abuses. Political "states of emergency," when rulers use reasons of necessity or threat to justify suspension of rights and representation, exemplify extreme manifestations of the security rationale (or rationalization) for blanket suspension of domestic freedoms within nation-states. Human rights defenders themselves are targeted as threats by some states.[27]

---

[27] Kenneth Roth, "The Abusers' Reaction: Intensifying Attacks on Human Rights Defenders, Organizations, and Institutions," *Brown Journal of World Affairs* 16, no. 2 (Spring/Summer 2010): 15–26.

In such situations, the justice of neighborhood is helpful, but not sufficient. Repeated emergency response strains the capacity of the neighbor. Furthermore, it is difficult for emergency care to fully support the autonomy and agency of persons under threat. Lives and livelihoods are interrupted when subject to repeated or extended emergency. The justice of neighborhood may support the human rights of others in the breach but it cannot substitute for their own ability to exercise rights against political repression.

Law

Law is an essential tool for the political realization of justice because it provides a structured way to address patterns of violation. Treaties and other legal standards recognized by states enable transnational human rights actors to speak more directly and formally in their efforts to protect individuals from arbitrary abuses of power. Human rights advocates have worked hard, and largely succeeded, at building international legal standards.[28] These standards also undergird political mobilization for justice by people at the local and national levels on behalf of their own human rights.[29]

Law can be a crucial means for generalizing responses to urgency. Readers of Honig, cited earlier in the discussion of the justice of neighborhood, will recognize that she cautions against universal norms, which can "insulate us from the urgencies of contingency" that give rise to solidaristic political action.[30] If we look at the history

---

[28] The generation of legal norms is a focus of my earlier book: Clark, *Diplomacy of Conscience*.

[29] Beth Simmons, *Mobilizing for Human Rights: International Law in Domestic Politics* (Cambridge: Cambridge University Press, 2009).

[30] Honig, *Emergency Politics*, 113. Her comments are made in the context of a debate with Seyla Benhabib on the merits of cosmopolitan law that begins in Seyla Benhabib, Jeremy Waldron, Bonnie Honig, Will Kymlicka, and Robert Post,

of human rights practice, however, it can be argued that human rights law extends the habit and preparedness that are also tools of the justice of neighborhood. In a philosophical study of emergency measures, Elaine Scarry characterizes law itself as "a form of habit (regularizing and making customary certain procedures and rules)."[31] When employed constructively, this feature of law as established procedure helps to ensure that political responses to emergency uphold human rights.

Case-by-case efforts caused early human rights advocates to see law as a tool not only for relief but also monitoring and accountability. Stefanie Grant, who helped to develop AI's research department starting in the late 1960s, described in a 1996 interview what it was like to learn about patterns of abuses before the emergence of relatively comprehensive human rights norms in law. Grant recalled the process as, first, asking why widespread abuses were not illegal, and then apprehending that

> [I]t isn't illegal because we weren't aware that it was happening ... And so you have a moral principle which then finds that the practice it abhors is not ... expressly illegal. And so then you move toward ... creating new law, as a means of preventing. And then, you use that law as the basis of your work. And so, it's like ... climbing the stairs of your house.[32]

As Grant observed, law offered a way to address human rights abuses more comprehensively. Law was a tool that brought human rights justice, through human rights advocacy, into an explicitly political context. Today, human rights law helps to define what justice looks

---

Another Cosmopolitanism, The Berkeley Tanner Lectures (Oxford; New York: Oxford University Press, 2006).

[31] Elaine Scarry, *Thinking in an Emergency* (New York: W. W. Norton, 2011), 101.

[32] Stefanie Grant, interviewed by Ann Marie Clark, New York, May 14, 1996, as cited in Clark, *Diplomacy of Conscience*, 18.

like. As a tool for the political realization of justice, the development of legal approaches has given activists leverage on the playing field of politically powerful actors – nation-states, state agents, and allied sectors of society – whose actions or policies trample on less powerful individuals and groups. Human rights law establishes rights standards around which political and legal mobilization can occur. Law offers forms of procedural justice when rights are violated, including transitional justice: domestic and international prosecutions of past human rights violators as countries transition to democracy.[33]

A Human Rights Culture of Argument

Human rights language has become a prominent way of talking about justice issues in global politics, so much so that it can be identified as a second tool in the political realization of justice. I call this discourse the human rights culture of argument. *Culture* refers to the widespread and common use of human rights language as part of political arguments related to justice concerns. Culture of *argument* refers to the shared expectation, within this culture, that political actors – states, political leaders, and non-state entities with material impact on the conditions of politics, such as business actors – justify their behavior in terms that refer to human rights. Law and legal argument have emerged as a strong component of human rights talk, so much so that human

---

[33] Sikkink, *The Justice Cascade*; Hunjoon Kim and Kathryn Sikkink, "Explaining the Deterrence Effect of Human Rights Prosecutions for Transitional Countries," *International Studies Quarterly* 54, no. 4 (2010): 939–963; Geoff Dancy and Verónica Michel, "Human Rights Enforcement from Below: Private Actors and Prosecutorial Momentum in Latin America and Europe," *International Studies Quarterly* 60, no. 1 (2016): 173–188; Geoff Dancy, Bridget E. Marchesi, Tricia D. Olsen, et al., "Behind Bars and Bargains: New Findings on Transitional Justice in Emerging Democracies," *International Studies Quarterly* 63, no. 1 (2019): 99–110.

rights norms themselves have become essential ways that justice is recognized.

In adopting the idea of a culture of argument as a way of observing the emergence of human rights language in political appeals for justice, I am indebted to the work of James Boyd White, the scholar of classics and law. White uses "culture of argument" to refer to conventions in the conduct of argumentation. In a memorable essay entitled, "The Dissolution of Meaning," White probes changes in what had been a shared standard of justification among adversaries in ancient Athens' diplomatic system, as recounted in Thucydides' *History of the Peloponnesian War*.[34] White reads Thucydides as an account of deterioration in the culture of argument: the weakening of respect for common standards of justice and fairness in the ancient Athenian world of roughly twenty-four centuries ago. He offers a bleak view of how appeals to justice, which appear as speeches in Thucydides' history, were gradually drained of significance in the face of power. The discourse of mutual justification reaches its nadir in the tragic encounter between Athens and the small island of Melos. Athens takes the island by force after denying the relevance of the Melians' appeals to justice, coldly admonishing their weaker adversaries that "right, as the world goes, is only in question between equals in power."[35]

White reads Athens' dismissal of Melos as an indicator of the "dissolution of meaning" that accompanies Athens' flagrant use of power and portends its eventual defeat. In contrast, I suggest that we can observe a different trajectory for human rights as a culture of

---

[34] James Boyd White, "The Dissolution of Meaning: Thucydides' History of His World," in *When Words Lose Their Meaning: Constitutions and Reconstitutions of Language, Character, and Community*, 59–92 (Chicago: University of Chicago Press, 1984).

[35] The Melian Dialogue, in Book 5 of Thucydides, *Complete Writings: The Peloponnesian War*, translated by Richard Crawley (New York: Modern Library, 1951).

argument in political relations. White has traced a grim trajectory in Thucydides' depiction of the opposition between principle and expediency but, as an empirical proposition about how a culture deteriorates, White's depiction implicitly poses an interesting hypothetical reversal. If an identifiable culture of argument can degenerate in observable ways, a trajectory of generation rather than deterioration of arguments conducive to appeals for justice might also occur.

We can investigate a trajectory of change in human rights appeals as a culture of argument about justice versus power. Transnational human rights appeals often rely on norm-based reasoning. The language used by human rights actors likely shapes and is shaped by historical continuities and traditions, as well as the emergence of newly recognized or newly contested issues, new law, and emerging norms – that is, new understandings of appropriate state behavior as defined by human rights law.[36] This view will inform my analysis of changes in the language of UA appeals for human rights by AI in Chapter 5 and in Oxfam's use of human rights language in Chapter 6.

For White, a culture of argument is constituted as "the discourse, the conventions of argument and action, by which [actors] maintain and regulate their relations with each other."[37] In this view, argumentation occurs within a broader tradition and mutually recognized, although often implicit, rules and expectations for adjudicating differences. The dynamics of a culture of argument emerge as actors take positions and make requests on contentious issues, revealing regularities and changes in their use of language.[38]

---

[36] Here I refer to the definition of international norms as "standards of appropriate behavior for actors with a given identity," in Martha Finnemore and Kathryn Sikkink, "International Norm Dynamics and Political Change," *International Organization* 52, no. 4 (Autumn 1998): 891.

[37] White, "The Dissolution of Meaning," 59.

[38] Ibid., see especially 59, 67, 89, 89 n.41 (303).

Not only in law but in life, "our language is in constant flux," as White has said in other work, so that propositions incorporated in speech and writing can themselves be thought of as practices.[39] I use White's conceptual approach to a culture of argument – understanding the "conventions of argument and action, by which [actors] maintain and regulate their relations with each other" – as a departure point for a more systematic identification of patterns of appeal to justice in AI's UA alerts. For all the mismatch between advocates and power-holders, the story of human rights activism in the late twentieth and early twenty-first centuries is in part a story of the emergence of arguments informed by human rights as new, and newly concrete, standards for justice in international politics. Terms of argument are characteristic of an emerging global discourse.[40] According to Frost and Lechner, one way to recognize a practice is that participants use a "common language of claims and counter-claims," even though they may, for various reasons, disagree on a set of ideals or goals.[41]

To explore the relationship between law and the culture of argument in this second vantage point on justice, I analyze the language of the series of AI's UA appeals from 1975 to 2007, with a view to how the language of law and concern changed over time. We can learn about the process of justice-seeking by studying this array of regular, publicly accessible claims made globally with reference to very specific circumstances in which individuals and groups find themselves.

---

[39] James Boyd White, *Justice as Translation: An Essay in Cultural and Legal Criticism* (Chicago: University of Chicago Press, 1990), 32–33.

[40] See also Thomas Risse, "'Let's Argue!': Communicative Action in World Politics," *International Organization* 54, no. 1 (Winter 2000): 1–39.

[41] Frost and Lechner, "Understanding International Practices from the Internal Point of View," 313.

In a multiyear project carried out as an archival and research collaboration with Amnesty International USA and my home university library's digital unit, the research team digitized and coded the UA document texts according to a set of indicators related to various justice-related aspects of human rights claims.[42] Using the coding data, in Chapter 5 I trace the increasing relevance of global human rights law to AI's globally disseminated arguments on behalf of specific individuals at risk. Amnesty International also pressed increasingly for accountability, frequently using the language of bringing perpetrators to justice. Although AI does cite local legal concerns throughout, I find that law at the global level appears more frequently in the alerts as time goes on. As more global law enters into force over time, however, the expression of care in the documents is a relative constant. In this form of human rights appeal, global justice-seeking resources for human rights have become increasingly specific with regard to law as part of the culture of argument, while retaining the expression of concern as part of participation in human rights politics.

The Integration of Social Justice with Human Rights

The integration of social justice as an object of human rights advocacy is the third component of justice that I consider. Social justice concerns include economic and distributive equality, global solidarity, and economic, social, and cultural (ESC) rights. When considering the origins and history of the human rights movement, social justice is an obvious, challenging test case for the range of human rights practice with regard to justice.

---

[42] Ann Marie Clark, P.I. and Paul Bracke, co-P.I., "Human Rights Texts for Digital Research: Archiving and Analyzing Amnesty International's Historic "Urgent Action" Bulletins at Purdue University" (Office of the Vice President for Research, Purdue University, award no. 206400, 2012). Additional advice and consultation was also provided by records staff at AI's International Secretariat in London.

The historian Samuel Moyn has posited that the focus of the traditional human rights framework on civil and political rights in the twentieth century, rooted as it was in liberal individualist understandings of rights, displaced the human rights movement's pursuit of greater economic and structural equality through politics.[43] Moyn pinpoints the 1970s as the beginning of the modern human rights movement, but Steven L. B. Jensen disputes this framing, as well as the finality of Moyn's argument about broader structural concerns in the development of global human rights politics.[44]

A view of the human rights movement of the 1970s should be regarded in a wider context. Kathryn Sikkink describes a long history of attention to democracy and human rights by Latin American jurists and diplomats, and others from the global South, including their contributions to the United Nations (UN) Charter and the Universal Declaration of Human Rights.[45] Jensen credits action by diplomats from the Global South, and Jamaica in particular, related to the politics of decolonization and racial justice, with "rekindling" attention to human rights at the UN in the early 1960s.[46] Events in the 1970s consolidated AI's visibility and

---

[43] Samuel Moyn, *The Last Utopia: Human Rights in History* (Cambridge, MA: Belknap Press of Harvard University Press, 2010); Samuel Moyn, *Not Enough: Human Rights in an Unequal World* (Cambridge, MA: Belknap Press of Harvard University Press, 2018).

[44] See Steven L. B. Jensen, *The Making of International Human Rights: The 1960s, Decolonization and the Reconstruction of Global Values* (Cambridge: Cambridge University Press, 2016), 11.

[45] Kathryn Sikkink, *Evidence for Hope: Making Human Rights Work in the 21st Century* (Princeton, NJ: Princeton University Press, 2017). See especially chapter 3, "The Diverse Political Origins of Human Rights," 55–93.

[46] See especially chapter 4, "From Jamaica with Law: The Rekindling of International Human Rights, 1962–1967," in Jensen, *The Making of International Human Rights*, 69–102.

influence, but the actors and concerns relevant to AI's founding had much earlier origins, as Tom Buchanan has demonstrated.[47] The civil and political human rights focus promoted by AI and Human Rights Watch in their advocacy and global legal standard-setting became prominent in that period,[48] but their approaches were not static. Others have suggested that human rights advocacy may reach its limits – not because it is too focused on political as opposed to economic rights but because it has not focused enough on levers of political power.[49] My view, based on the research I present later in the book on the incorporation of rights arguments in development-sector advocacy, is that the practical strength and broad adaptability of rights arguments may yet extend to new ways of securing economic and social justice.[50]

As traditional human rights groups in the 1990s were still questioning what they should do about social justice, development sector NGOs engaged in emergency aid and advocacy that they hoped would mitigate the effects of unjust economic structures. They saw a place for rights arguments in their own work. The importance of aid in emergency remained, but their dissatisfaction with charity stemmed precisely from its inability to address political and economic inequalities, and international economic policies, that they saw as

---

[47] Tom Buchanan, *Amnesty International and Human Rights Activism in Postwar Britain, 1945–1977* (Cambridge: Cambridge University Press, 2020).

[48] Human Rights Watch was founded in the early 1990s, but was made up of regional Watch Committees that formed in the 1970s. See Aryeh Neier, "Human Rights Watch," in *The International Human Rights Movement: A History*, 204–232 (Princeton, NJ: Princeton University Press, 2012).

[49] For a selection of essays that includes rich debate on these concerns, see Stephen Hopgood, Jack Snyder, and Leslie Vinjamuri, eds., *Human Rights Futures* (Cambridge: Cambridge University Press, 2017).

[50] See also Ann Marie Clark, "What Kind of Justice for Human Rights?," in *Human Rights and Justice: Philosophical, Economic, and Social Perspectives*, eds. Melissa Labonte and Kurt Mills, 14–32 (Abingdon-on-Thames: Routledge, 2018).

exacerbating poverty. To address the problem, Oxfam was an early conceptual author of what Paul Nelson and Ellen Dorsey termed "new rights advocacy," the integration of human rights concepts by NGOs in the economic and social development sector.[51] Oxfam and other groups with an expert understanding of poverty began to converge on human rights to support calls for economic and social justice.

Oxfam saw rights as providing the political leverage needed in global efforts against poverty. Human rights practice offers a number of emergent tools for social justice. As a matter of solidarity, human rights tools protect the political agency and well-being of people subject to structural injustice.[52] The human rights culture of argument permits the use of political rights against discrimination of all kinds. Moves to protect human rights defenders from discrimination as rights defenders, rather than as defenders of certain kinds of rights, for example, potentially bring activists on a variety of issues more directly under the protection of global human rights law. A second emergent tool is the development of ways to assert global ESC rights in specific local contexts, in line with a "bottom up" approach to the interpretation of rights norms.[53] Sally Engle Merry's discussion of the translations of rights into vernacular arguments in the pursuit of women's human rights is one example.[54] Scholarship on women's movements, in which so many ESC rights come into play, demonstrate women's leadership in these areas of

---

[51] Paul J. Nelson and Ellen Dorsey, *New Rights Advocacy: Changing Strategies of Development and Human Rights NGOs* (Washington, DC: Georgetown University Press, 2008); Junhyup Kim, "To Give or to Act? The Transition of NGOs from Aid Donors to Human Rights Advocates" (PhD dissertation, Purdue University, 2018).

[52] Anna Carella and Brooke Ackerly, "Ignoring Rights Is Wrong: Re-politicizing Gender Equality and Development with the Rights-Based Approach," *International Feminist Journal of Politics* 19, no. 2 (2017): 137–152.

[53] Shareen Hertel, "Re-framing Human Rights Advocacy: The Rise of Economic Rights," in *Human Rights Futures*, eds. Stephen Hopgood, Jack Snyder, and Leslie Vinjamuri (Cambridge: Cambridge University Press, 2017), 238.

[54] Merry, *Human Rights and Gender Violence*.

advocacy.[55] In another realm, Shareen Hertel documents the politics of including the rights of local stakeholders when considering the impact of global business concerns.[56]

Despite the widespread move to human rights by NGOs in the development sector, heated debate over the strategies and capacities of global human rights organizations themselves emerged in the early part of this millennium. Kenneth Roth, the head of Human Rights Watch, explained in 2004 why his organization was then sticking mainly with civil and political rights advocacy for pragmatic and theoretical reasons.[57] He argued that the tools of legal advocacy are not well suited to demands that states reallocate resources; instead, a better strategy was to push for antidiscrimination protections that had implications for such claims. The classic human rights strategy depends on clear identification of "violator, violation, and remedy." Accordingly, Roth argued, although human rights NGOs like Human Rights Watch could in principle support calls for ESC rights, their leverage would be weak in the absence of such clarity. Roth referred to a standard political theory of rights and duties to back his argument about how NGOs' power and resources should best be applied: the nature of ESC rights claims makes it much more difficult to assign special, specific obligations to states – that is, blame, and specific responsibility for fulfillment.[58]

---

[55] Elisabeth Jay Friedman, "Gendering the Agenda: The Impact of the Transnational Women's Rights Movement at the UN Conferences of the 1990s," *Women's Studies International Forum* 26, no. 4 (2003): 313–331; Mala Htun and S. Laurel Weldon, *The Logics of Gender Justice: State Action on Women's Rights around the World* (Cambridge: Cambridge University Press, 2018); Ackerly, *Just Responsibility*.

[56] Shareen Hertel, *Tethered Fates: Companies, Communities, and Rights at Stake* (Oxford: Oxford University Press, 2019).

[57] Kenneth Roth, "Defending Economic, Social and Cultural Rights: Practical Issues Faced by an International Human Rights Organization," *Human Rights Quarterly* 26, no. 1 (2004): 63–73.

[58] See also Onora O'Neill, "The Dark Side of Human Rights," *International Affairs* 81, no. 2 (2005): 433.

This last debate brings into relief the question whether the difficulties of a rights approach to address ESC rights more directly portend a critical failure of human rights as tools of justice. However, the potential for human rights tools within a diversity of justice conceptions may be obscured by a one-size view of rights logic. Among human rights NGOs, political tensions arise from differences in priority, preferred strategy, and power. Such tensions are all the more visible, and become more productive, when understood as indicators of where justice and human rights do not yet fit. Viewing the emergence and development of human rights politics in tandem with a justice lens shows remarkable creativity and accomplishment, as well as the way in which this tension may prompt change toward a better fit.

4

Expanding the Global Neighborhood

Amnesty International's Urgent Action

The story of transnational work to aid and protect individuals is the story of a widening domain of action since the 1960s. This chapter recounts how human rights advocates at Amnesty International (AI) devised what became a durable practice of appeals for people in human rights emergencies. Through its system of Urgent Action (UA) alerts, AI shared information with members who could then write messages on behalf of individuals threatened by egregious human rights violations in other countries.

Telling this story of how Urgent Action developed demonstrates how early human rights advocacy implemented three tools of the justice of neighborhood – active care, habit, and appeals – and became a bridge to further political realization of justice. The chapter begins with a focus on a critical period in the early 1970s, when AI transitioned from working only for people imprisoned for nonviolent speech or beliefs, protected as "human rights" in articles 18 and 19 of the Universal Declaration of Human Rights, to fighting to protect all people from torture and other forms of ill-treatment. This transition is what turned AI into a true human rights organization, and for this reason, it is first necessary to offer some background on the idiosyncrasies of AI as an organization. But the focus here is not on the organization per se, except as a context for the step-by-step actions of people who saw suffering and fixed their minds and skills on a way to help. Practical efforts like AI's Urgent Action are inherently imperfect and incomplete in their ability to achieve change. Therefore, it is important not to idealize this work, or the organization, but to use it to uncover an understanding of global justice work by observing emerging human rights practice.

In many cases, as studies of society's helpers tell us, what seem in retrospect to be significant achievements in the human response to need emerge in an ordinary way, when those individuals meet with a call for help and respond.[1] It can be a challenge to incorporate this perspective into an understanding of the contributions of human rights work in global politics, but it is theoretically and empirically crucial to do so. One reason human rights practices deserve to be theorized with regard to the pursuit of justice is that these early efforts established routine practices that could make a difference when repeated again and again. In this way, the ostensibly heroic part of justice work can be parsed and becomes approachable. Human rights work by professionals in nongovernmental organizations (NGOs), and by other activists and allies, emerges through daily engagement with problems in the world. Their activities can be mined for a practical understanding of the elements of justice.

Background: From Fighting Unjust Imprisonment to Urgent Action against Torture

By the time AI was ten years old, in 1971, its primary contribution to transnational human rights activism had been its advocacy for people it

---

[1] For example, François Rochat and Andre Modigliani, "The Ordinary Quality of Resistance: From Milgram's Laboratory to the Village of Le Chambon," *Journal of Social Issues* 51, no. 3 (1995): 195–210; Ervin Staub, "The Psychology of Bystanders, Perpetrators, and Heroic Helpers," in *The Psychology of Good and Evil: Why Children, Adults, and Groups Help and Harm Others*, ed. Ervin Staub, 291–324 (Cambridge: Cambridge University Press, 2003).

identified as prisoners of conscience. Amnesty International used this term to refer to people imprisoned for expression of their political, religious, or other beliefs, who had not used or advocated violence.[2] Amnesty International's identification with work for prisoners of conscience had begun with a 1961 *Times* (London) appeal in support of six such prisoners in Czechoslovakia, Hungary, Portugal, Romania, Spain, and the USA. Its ambitions and popular membership had grown quickly.[3]

To combat a particular kind of injustice – unjust imprisonment as a punishment for exercise of freedom of speech about matters of conscience such as political or religious beliefs – AI assigned each prisoner of conscience to a local AI group. The process was called "adopting" a prisoner. An adoption group would press for humane conditions of detention, due process of law or other procedural issues where appropriate, and the person's eventual release. Most groups met at least monthly. Members would correspond with relevant officials (as suggested by AI) by postal mail and sometimes by telephone or telegram, to indicate concern about the prisoners' well-being, send messages of support directly to the prisoners themselves and their loved ones where possible, and sometimes offer forms of material support to detainees' families.

[2] On prisoners of conscience, see Edy Kaufman, "Prisoners of Conscience: The Shaping of a New Human Rights Concept," *Human Rights Quarterly* 13, no. 3 (1991): 339–367.

[3] Benenson, "The Forgotten Prisoners"; and see Buchanan, "The Truth Will Set You Free." Amnesty International leadership and staff also engaged in more political relations, much of which remained behind the scenes in the early days. See ibid.; Buchanan, *Amnesty International and Human Rights Activism in Postwar Britain*; Clark, *Diplomacy of Conscience*; Swati Srivastava, "Navigating NGO–Government Relations in Human Rights: New Archival Evidence from Amnesty International, 1961–1986," *International Studies Quarterly* (2021).

The prisoner adoption model formed the core of AI's work in its first ten-plus years. Several features of prisoner adoption are notable within a justice framework. First, this activity was deliberately transnational. Groups were not assigned to work for prisoners in their own countries. Second, after AI identified and assigned prisoners of conscience cases, the groups were encouraged to be creative, and they had a great deal of discretion regarding how to advance the case. Group members sometimes formed close ties to the prisoners and their families. Third, AI emphasized political impartiality by seeking to balance adoptions from countries of every political stripe. The model in the early days was for each group to manage three adoption cases: one from the West; one from the Eastern Bloc countries; and one from the Global South. The guiding principle was the right to nonviolent exercise of freedom of conscience. The robustness of the process depended on active care by lay members of AI, not the experts, to secure measures of justice and well-being for the prisoners that they had adopted.

The Urgency of Human Rights Action

The adoption model forged strong links between AI and its membership, and between members and the people AI were trying to assist, but staffers and grassroots members began to see its limitations. Countries' repressive practices were changing. For example, agents of repression in countries like Brazil, Guatemala, Chile, and Argentina, all countries that AI was covering by the early 1970s, were employing torture, severe ill-treatment, political killings, and disappearances. All could occur quickly and separately from acknowledged detention. The information AI researchers were gathering about the treatment of prisoners across the world – through general tracking and reporting on political conditions and repression in individual countries, and through its unique, focused inquiries on behalf of individual prisoners – indicated an urgent need to address dire violations of persons' physical and psychological integrity within and outside of the prison cell. Amnesty International's growing concern about the use of violent repressive tactics, beyond simple political imprisonment, propelled the creation and development of a new approach to urgent cases.

In practical terms, the adoption model was proving difficult to "scale up" as AI attracted more members and more national branches, called sections. Amnesty International has always been composed of independent, national sections, but its policies, its country-level research, and its case work for individuals were organized centrally at the International Secretariat. Information was gathered by staffers in the research department. They monitored multiple countries at a time, communicating with in-country contacts, with political exiles, and other country experts, including exceptionally skilled volunteers who maintained their own contacts in repressive countries. Amnesty International's growth created demand that groups be matched with new cases that they could work on, but prisoner adoption required careful verification of a person's status as a prisoner of conscience, which could be time-consuming. Even discounting the time required for the verification process, prisoner adoption was too slow to counter changes in repressive techniques. The group-directed correspondence process entailed by adoption could not prevent initial, often serious mistreatment of detainees.

In addition, there was a question of moral consistency. Torture, political killings, and disappearances were objectionable whether or not a person met all of the criteria designating a prisoner of conscience. Nor were such tactics used only inside the prison cell. If AI was truly concerned about mistreatment while in detention, why should its concern be limited only to those who qualified as prisoners of conscience?

To supplement its trademark focus on prisoners of conscience, AI decided to pursue general thematic work opposing torture in all circumstances.[4] The Campaign for the Abolition of Torture (CAT), a research and action program now recognized as a landmark endeavor, was launched in 1973 with a report on use of torture across the world.[5] The campaign culminated in a trailblazing international conference on torture hosted by AI in December 1974.[6] As the planned campaign came to an end, AI created a permanent CAT department at the International Secretariat.

As part of the antitorture campaign, AI experimented with a new Urgent Action technique. Urgent Action was an innovation on its transnational grassroots advocacy model that would complement prisoner of conscience adoption but would, it was hoped, aid more individuals more quickly. The idea for Urgent Action came out of AI's work on Brazil, which had been taken up by a new staffer, Tracy Ulltveit-Moe, in 1971.

Ulltveit-Moe had applied for a research position in response to an ad in the *Times* (London).[7] She had been educated as a political scientist at Stanford and Columbia University, with a focus on Latin America. Amnesty International was strengthening its focus on that region and especially Brazil, a former Portuguese colony then entering its seventh year of repressive military rule. A *Times* advertisement from June 16, 1971, which may be the one Ulltveit-Moe answered, casts a wide net (see Figure 4.1).

---

[4] Clark, *Diplomacy of Conscience.*

[5] Amnesty International, *Report on Torture* (London: Duckworth, in association with Amnesty International Publications, 1973).

[6] Clark, *Diplomacy of Conscience*, 53–54.

[7] Tracy Ulltveit-Moe, interviewed by Ann Marie Clark, London, May 15, 2013.

AMNESTY INTERNATIONAL research department requires researchers or research assistants in the following areas: (1) Latin America, (2) United States, (3) Eastern Europe, (4) Asia with special reference to south Asia, i.e., India, Pakistan, etc. Applicants should have a good knowledge of their respective regions and the appropriate linguistic qualifications. In the case of the Latin American post knowledge of Portuguese is essential, salary £1,560 researcher, £1,100 assistant researcher. Closing date for application 5th July, 1971. Amnesty, Turnagain Lane, Farringdon St., E.C.4.

Source: *The Times* (London), classified advertisement, June 16, 1971, p. 23. Facsimile on file with the author.

Figure 4.1 Text of Amnesty International newspaper advertisement seeking researchers, 1971.

Ulltveit-Moe arrived at the starting point of a period of major growth and change at AI. Human rights violations in Latin America were intensifying as authoritarian military regimes continued to carry out counterinsurgency policies. Amnesty International's headquarters then housed only about twenty people, according to Ulltveit-Moe, and covered a limited number of countries. Many support tasks, such as newspaper searches for current information on country situations and political arrests, were carried out by volunteers. Single researchers could be responsible for monitoring the human rights situations of whole regions.

Ulltveit-Moe's portfolio as a researcher included, in addition to Brazil, Portugal, Lusophone (Portuguese-speaking) Africa, and all of Latin America:

> When I tell people that, they think that it was incredible. But in fact, ... the person who had the job before me ... was responsible in theory, for the research of all countries that spoke

Latin-derived languages ... it gives you an idea how small the secretariat was.[8]

Being an AI researcher on a country where serious repression was occurring involved more than passive monitoring. The work required careful political judgment and analysis based on active communication, where possible, with knowledgeable observers, NGOs located inside the country, expatriates who may have fled the repression, and with the families or colleagues of people who were direct targets of repression.

Brazil had been under authoritarian military rule since 1964. It was a relatively early adopter of a US-backed Cold War counterinsurgency doctrine in Latin America that prescribed the use of extreme measures against suspected subversives. Similar patterns were present or soon emerged across the region. Suspected political opponents of the government were being abducted or arrested, brutally tortured, and sometimes killed by agents of the military government.[9] Military police and agents of the security forces used a sequenced system of brutality, including an elaborate terminology referring to various torture methods. Brazil's 2014 truth commission report confirmed that at least 1,843 persons had been tortured between 1964 and 1977; over 6,300 alleged incidents of torture, in total, were reported by those individuals.[10] This estimate was thought to be conservative.

---

[8] Ibid.

[9] Peter Kornbluh, "Brazil: Torture Techniques Revealed in Declassified U.S. Documents," National Security Archive, George Washington University (July 8, 2014), https://nsarchive2.gwu.edu/NSAEBB/NSAEBB478/.

[10] Brazil, Comissão Nacional da Verdade (CNV) [National Truth Commission], *Relatório da Comissão Nacional da Verdade*, vol. 1 (Brasilia: CNV, 2014), 349, http://cnv.memoriasreveladas.gov.br/images/pdf/relatorio/volume_1_digital.pdf; citing Arquidiocese de São Paulo [Archdiocese of São Paulo], *Projeto "Brasil: nunca mais,"* vol. 1 (São Paulo: Arquidiocese de São Paulo, 1985), Projeto A, tomo V, 13–15, 70, http://bnmdigital.mpf.mp.br/pt-br/.

Amnesty International sent a small mission of inquiry to Brazil in April and May of 1972 to gather information on torture. Its *Report on Allegations of Torture in Brazil* was published in September 1972. The Brazil entry in AI's annual report for 1972–1973 noted that even more information came to AI after the report, possibly because of its notoriety in Brazil.[11]

Brazilian expatriates were essential sources of information on what was happening in Brazil. According to Ulltveit-Moe, German AI members as well as Brazilian expats in Germany and elsewhere in Europe were pressing AI to do more than "identify and adopt" prisoners. Amnesty International was in touch with a community of Brazilian expatriates in Chile,[12] and with Brazilian expats in Europe.[13] A further supplement to AI's information came from a network of AI member experts, called Coordination Groups, who shared information from their in-country contacts with the research department.[14] Expatriates with firsthand knowledge of the torture practices of Brazilian authorities were asking what AI could do about it.

Amnesty International had begun assigning so-called investigation cases to adoption groups. These were cases in which more research had to be done before AI could be sure that a person matched its criteria for prisoner-of-conscience status. As mentioned, investigations could be slow. According to what Ulltveit-Moe was hearing from her contacts as a Brazil researcher, AI's standard approach was "not acceptable to those sectors like the exiles and the membership that were concerned about this" because prisoners were being severely mistreated

---

[11] Amnesty International, *Report on Allegations of Torture in Brazil* (London: Amnesty International Publications, 1972); Amnesty International, "Brazil," in *Annual Report 1972–73*, 46–47 (London: Amnesty International Publications, 1973).

[12] Amnesty International, "Brazil," 47.

[13] Tracy Ulltveit-Moe, interviewed by Ann Marie Clark, telephone, January 22, 2018.

[14] See, for example, Amnesty International, "Brazil," 47.

before anything could be done. Their message was "You've got to do more on this!"[15]

Despite the sense, shared by many staff, that AI needed to do more to oppose violent tactics of repression, its apolitical identity was linked to the prisoner-of-conscience concept, which many felt was difficult to manipulate politically and therefore key to AI's legitimacy. Exiles and people committed to political resistance in countries affected by repression frequently did not share the same nonpartisan stance. The constraints imposed by AI's working principles made it difficult to meet the realities of how torture was being carried out, and therefore, difficult to advocate for people affected by torture.

A few staffers at AI called an informal weekend meeting to discuss the situation in Brazil in early 1972. These sorts of meetings took place occasionally, as researchers considered action in particular circumstances, but this one held particular weight. Not only was AI planning its first ever "campaign" on a single country in response to the situation in Brazil,[16] it was also growing increasingly concerned about torture. The group was small: Ulltveit-Moe, Martin Ennals, then-Secretary-General of AI, Maggie Beirne, a staff assistant then working with Ulltveit-Moe, and a Brazilian lawyer, Annina Alcantara de Carvalho.[17] Carvalho was an outspoken Brazilian expatriate, based in Paris, who herself had been arrested and threatened with torture before deciding to leave the country.[18]

Researchers were seeing a pattern in Brazil, according to Ulltveit-Moe, that "[now] you see, and we saw subsequently, all over the place," that "the principal human rights problem in Brazil was that people were being arrested and tortured in the first 48 hours after detention."[19] As Brazil's truth commission later reported, people were

---

[15] Ulltveit-Moe, January 22, 2018. [16] Ibid. [17] Ulltveit-Moe, May 15, 2013.
[18] John Young, "Brazilian Torture Cases," *Times*, March 24, 1971.
[19] Ulltveit-Moe, May 15, 2013.

tortured first and interrogated afterward ... which was [thought to be] favorable for extracting confessions that would catch the greatest number of persons in the net of repression.[20]

A sense of justice combined with AI's potential capabilities called for action. The urgency of torture threats challenged AI's practice of vetting the details of an affected person's political history, which effectively prevented timely intervention. Discussion at the meeting involved struggling not just with what to do but how to do it in a way that maintained the core principles that AI members could support, according to Ulltveit-Moe.

At the meeting, Ulltveit-Moe proposed that AI take up a new form of action. They needed a new kind of action with a name that made it clear that "we have a very, very urgent concern" without implying anything about whether the affected person was necessarily a prisoner of conscience: Urgent Action.[21] Amnesty International could issue short, quick alerts on cases of individuals under threat. Alerts would call on members to act right away, based on its knowledge of impending threats to a specified individual.

In April 1972, prior to the launch of CAT, AI's international governing body, the International Executive Committee (IEC), approved a test of Urgent Action appeals with relation to the situation in Brazil. At the September meeting of the IEC, Ulltveit-Moe reported that, "in view of the internal situations in Latin American countries," AI should accept that "the likely emphasis will be on torture reports and so on, rather than prisoner of conscience work." The high levels of internal conflict and "government repression of a particularly brutal nature," including the systematic

---

[20] Roman Catholic Archdiocese of Sao Paulo (Brazil), *Torture in Brazil: A Report by the Archdiocese of São Paulo* [*Brasil: Nunca Mais*], trans. Jaime Wright, ed. Joan Dassin (New York: Vintage Books, 1986), 69–70.

[21] Ulltveit-Moe, May 15, 2013.

use of torture and other violence, would make it difficult to maintain AI's prisoner-of-conscience model.[22]

The first UA appeal was issued in 1973 on behalf of Luiz Basilio Rossi, a Brazilian professor of economics. Many years later, AI reported his description of how it affected his situation: "I knew that my case had become public, I knew they could no longer kill me. Then the pressure on me decreased and conditions improved."[23] The first published mention of an "urgent action campaign" appears in the "Brazil" entry of AI's 1972–1973 annual report:

> [C]oordination groups were asked to organize letter-writing campaigns on behalf of persons whom (*sic*), it is feared, are being tortured, but about whom too little is known to ascertain whether or not they could be considered prisoners of conscience.[24]

The success of initial Urgent Actions for cases in Brazil created optimism about the potential for broader use of UA appeals. According to Ulltveit-Moe, her colleague in the newly permanent CAT department, Leah Dover-Fleming, reached out to discuss Urgent Action as the new department's agenda was being planned.[25] Once AI had decided to incorporate Urgent Action as a continuing part of its repertoire, Dover-Fleming set up the format and the system for distribution to a few national sections from the International Secretariat, said Dick Oosting. Oosting had first worked for the Dutch section of AI during the initial campaign, and came to London to head the CAT department, later called simply the campaign department, in 1974. According to Oosting,

---

[22] Amnesty International, "International Executive Committee, Meeting in Utrecht, 6–7 September 1972. Research and Action, Item 9," Amsterdam: International Institute for the Study of Social History, Amnesty International, International Secretariat Archives. Document location: ARCH00200, Inv. No. 51, Folder 51, 1972, 7.

[23] Amnesty International, "AI@50: The Amnesty International Timeline" (2011). http://static.amnesty.org/ai50/ai50-amnesty-international-timeline.pdf.

[24] Amnesty International, "Brazil," 47. [25] Ulltveit-Moe, January 22, 2018.

the Urgent Action process "was developed very quickly into quite an efficient machinery."[26]

Patricia Feeney, the AI researcher on Argentina in the late 1970s, recalled the period as demanding "intense, immediate" action. Amnesty International's new Urgent Action network played a "critical" role in Argentina,

> because we knew with disappearances, or we believed, that if you didn't get people released within 48 hours, they would be dead. Really, the chances of survival were nil. Or, very low . . . And so these hordes, you know, waves of letters would come raining out of the sky from all around the world.[27]

Feeney recounted that the appeals also offered "some support and comfort to the families and the human rights movement that, you know, Amnesty was trying to do *something*."[28]

Making the technique a permanent part of AI's action repertoire marked a significant change in the scope and speed of AI's ability to make transnational appeals to justice for individuals. Amnesty International viewed a positive, unimpeachable reputation as part of its resources for mobilization on behalf of selected cases. Yet, there was a hope that AI could and should move public opinion further, by acting for more complex cases that were arguably in line with a firm philosophical and moral high ground against human rights abuses, and with AI's habit of framing its reasons for action according to moral and legal principles. These discussions, and decisions to work on torture, on other kinds of violations, were part of a bridge to AI's additional

---

[26] Dick Oosting, interviewed by Ann Marie Clark, Bussum, the Netherlands, January 30, 2018.

[27] Patricia Feeney, interviewed by Ann Marie Clark, online via Zoom, June 1, 2020. Feeney remained at AI until 1990, then moved to Oxfam to work on development and human rights issues, as discussed in Chapter 5.

[28] Ibid.

work on international legal principles. Amnesty International's first legal officer, Nigel Rodley, who joined AI staff at about the same time as Ulltveit-Moe, helped to build this bridge.[29]

The shift to Urgent Action holds lessons about the push for justice and the tension between rules and human needs. The extension of active care for some political prisoners created an increased sensitivity to what justice demands. Although adoption was explicitly concerned with extending concern and care for prisoners, as well as advocating for them with government officials, the potential for timely expressions of concern was diminished because of AI's demanding adoption criteria. Delay meant further possible harm to detainees, it meant excluding many people from potential relief, and it entailed sitting by while severe harms were inflicted on people that AI might be able to protect. The sense of justice – "you've got to do more!" – was compelling.

The Urgent Action Network: Amnesty International USA and the Development of the Network

Amnesty International's structure, of course, was based on local groups of members in a number of countries. As mentioned, initial alerts had been sent through the coordination groups, who were, in essence, a set of super-volunteers. It fell to national sections to fully develop this form of action throughout the regular membership.

The US national organization of AI, which became large and prominent among national AI sections, was still comparatively small in the early 1970s. A number of local adoption groups had been formed by the early 1970s, but the view from London was that the US section was not particularly robust. There was a sense from abroad that opposing the Vietnam war had absorbed the attention of many American

---

[29] Ulltveit-Moe, January 22, 2018; see also Clark, *Diplomacy of Conscience.*

political activists.[30] As it turns out, a US Vietnam veteran, Scott Harrison, picked up Urgent Action implementation in the USA. Harrison turned the Urgent Action response into a practical routine, never losing sight of the fact that every UA alert could prevent or lessen mistreatment of specific individuals elsewhere in the world. He built and developed the Urgent Action network in the USA from 1975 until his retirement in 2006, when operations were moved to the Washington, DC office of Amnesty International USA.

Harrison had volunteered for the Marines as a seventeen-year-old just out of high school. He was eighteen by the time he was inducted in 1967. After a short period of special training, Harrison was sent to Vietnam with the expectation that he would be stationed in a village as an interpreter. That assignment never materialized.

> When we went over there, we were supposed to be interpreters and interrogators. And when we got there, there were so many Marines being killed at the DMZ that we were just sent up there to replace.[31] So, I was a machine gunner. I thought I was going over there with a pistol, and was like a Peace Corps-type person, you know.[32]

In sum, "we were flown in as a graduating class to Danang, and they didn't need those people anymore. They needed more grunts on the front lines." Harrison was wounded in battle and hospitalized. As a result, he was sent home with an honorable discharge after seven months of service.

The experience had a profound effect on Harrison. Vietnam was "a slap in the face. There was more happening here than what you were told in your suburban high school outside Dallas." He began to

---

[30] Ulltveit-Moe, May 15, 2013.

[31] DMZ refers to "demilitarized zone," the dividing line between South Vietnam and North Vietnam.

[32] Scott Harrison, interviewed by Ann Marie Clark, Nederland, CO, July 17, 2013. Unless otherwise noted, quotations that follow are drawn from the interview.

think more deeply about his experience and his relation to the world, but

> I also, at the same time, was totally traumatized. I was wounded, I was hospitalized, I had seen a lot of people die, my best friends died, so I was totally traumatized.

The return home, even though he had been away less than a year, was abrupt and disorienting. Upon discharge, "there was no cool-down period. I was in a hospital and then I came back." His sense of displacement was heightened by the politics back home:

> [T]he popular culture was against the war and against the veterans, really . . . I didn't have cruel treatment happen to me, but I had disinterest – in that, people would look away, when I had a military haircut, that sort of thing, . . . when I got discharged. So . . . there were all kinds of things going on in my head. I was depressed, I also couldn't fit in to the culture.

The experiences left Harrison wanting isolation, a sense that stayed with him while attending the University of Texas at Austin with the help of federal education benefits provided to veterans. After graduating in 1972, Harrison built a sailboat. "My motivation was to get away from the United States. I had my own problems with the post-Vietnam experience. So, I thought I just wanted to go away, and . . . I did that."

Harrison first lived on his boat in Sausalito, California, taking "a couple of different jobs" to pay for construction materials and day-to-day expenses. "And then I took off!" He sailed for parts of a year in the Pacific. Over a span of about two years, when not out to sea, he docked at guest berths along the California coast. Harrison said his escape "worked, but it only worked in terms of an escape, an isolation." After a while, he was through with that kind of isolation: "I mean, I enjoyed the ocean, whales, dolphins, all that stuff. But I'm not like that. I'm not a low-energy guy." There were times out on the ocean when

Harrison felt the urge, a kind of calling, to do something practical to make the world better. "Nothing mysterious, you know, but just to come back and do something."

In late spring of 1974, docking in Santa Cruz harbor, Harrison heard about a Joan Baez benefit concert and decided to attend. It was a benefit for AI, dedicated to human rights in Chile and especially to the memory of Victor Jara, a Chilean singer and writer who had been tortured and killed after the September 1973 coup in Chile.[33] Baez gave benefit concerts for various causes in that era, but was an especially strong supporter of AI.[34]

Amnesty International USA's first central office in the USA was in San Francisco, rather than in New York,[35] and at the concert, Baez announced that the San Francisco office of AI needed volunteers. Still living on his boat, Harrison thought about it for a while and "not right away, but eventually," he showed up to check out AI's San Francisco

---

[33] Anonymous, "Joan Baez Heads Benefit," *San Francisco Examiner*, May 23, 1974; Michele Lomax, "Jara Tribute to Feature Joan Baez," *San Francisco Examiner*, May 27, 1974. According to newspaper sources, the concert Harrison attended was likely the one held on May 29 at the First Congregational Church in San Francisco. Especially because Jara had been a singer and activist, a number of performers were holding benefit concerts for Chile in this period. Later, in 1976, Baez headlined a "Benefit for the Restoration of Human Rights in Chile" with Pete Seeger and others in New York. An image of the poster for the New York concert appears online in a blog posting at Elijah Wald, "Te Recuerdo Amanda," Old Friends: A Songobiography (songblog, August 27, 2016), www.elijahwald.com/songblog/te-recuerdo-amanda/.

[34] Along with Ginetta Sagan, an Italian who had been imprisoned under Mussolini and was involved with AI at the national and global level, Baez helped to found and develop AI groups on the West Coast. The first West Coast AI group met in Sagan's home outside San Francisco. Myrna Oliver, "Ginetta Sagan Dies; Torture Victim Fought for Political Prisoners," *Los Angeles Times*, August 30, 2000, www.latimes.com/archives/la-xpm-2000-aug-2030-mn-12538-story.html.

[35] Amnesty International USA, "Joan Baez: A Lifetime of Human Rights Advocacy" (2019), www.amnestyusa.org/joan-baez-a-lifetime-of-human-rights-advocacy/. For a time, Amnesty International USA had a loosely bicoastal structure centered around New York and San Francisco.

office in January 1975. The office was "a very stimulating place, lots of people running around, doing stuff. That turned me on. Because people were just busy and getting stuff done." He started volunteering regularly. In this milieu, not surprisingly, there was also lots of talk about political change. Harrison said he was less interested personally in "political discussions about changing things" than about doing the work of protecting individuals from government-sponsored repression. "I could work on one person at a time, see what I could do to help – what we could do, what I could do to facilitate."[36]

Shortly after he arrived at the office, Harrison met Ellen Moore, another new volunteer. Harrison and Moore clicked right away, and so began what would be a long personal and professional partnership. Moore's life, too, had been impacted by the Vietnam war. She was involved in the antiwar movement as a student in New York, and had married a fellow activist. When he was drafted, they had moved to Canada, where they made a living on a farm for several years. When the marriage ended, she moved to San Francisco, where she worked as a teacher and volunteered with AI.[37]

The Urgent Action network had yet to become part of AI's regular work in the USA. It was not really even a network. As the Urgent Actions were sent out of London to selected national offices, those offices had to figure out how best to distribute them. National sections had to improvise. In the San Francisco office, the Urgent Action network was assigned to Harrison as "something to try to figure out, you know, 'What can we do with these cases that keep coming from London on the telex terminal?'"[38] Moore recounted the story in more detail. Shortly after Harrison arrived in January 1975,

---

[36] Harrison, July 17, 2013.
[37] Ellen Moore, interviewed by Ann Marie Clark, Nederland, CO, July 17, 2013.
[38] Harrison, July 17, 2013.

> Janet [Johnstone], who was the office administrator, came to us, and she . . . had this shoebox of . . . little notes that she kept, and she said, "The International Secretariat is thinking about [trying out] in some sections this program, the Urgent Action Program," and she said, "What do you think about it?"[39]

The office was in a part of a triplex house in the city. They went to the kitchen to talk about it over coffee. They recognized that the process would entail

> a departure from prisoner work as we know it, but . . . we wondered, could it ever be fast enough? Well, given how slow everything at Amnesty was, it seemed *very* fast to get this information.[40]

The information would be sent by telex from the International Secretariat in London. The question was how to distribute it quickly. The idea was exciting, but Amnesty International USA had a limited budget for paid staff. And so, according to Moore, "[Scott] would have to do it . . . Immediately, his mind is going, 'How to quickly get this stuff out?'" In practical terms, that included putting together a way to get the telex duplicated, before computers, addressing and stuffing envelopes, keeping track of who would receive which Urgent Actions, and so forth. As the details were worked out, the mechanics were reviewed at staff meetings, and people would chime in with ideas. "But it was mostly him putting it together."[41] The equipment used then by the AI office, and many other activists, is mostly obsolete now: typewriter, mimeograph, ditto machine, and an "addressograph," a machine for addressing envelopes with a system of sortable, reusable metal cards. When an Urgent Action came in over the telex, information had to be typed up on a stencil for duplication on a mimeograph or ditto machine, printed, folded, put in the addressed envelopes, and mailed out. Said Moore,

---

[39] Moore, July 17, 2013. [40] Ibid. [41] Ibid.

Everybody helped. Everybody helped, even people with other jobs. The idea was, if we got a UA, it should go out that day.[42]

In the fall of 1975, Harrison was brought on staff with a salary of $100 per month, and assigned to coordinate the national Urgent Action network out of San Francisco.

When the Urgent Action network came, it just fit me to a tee, because the focus was on helping the individual . . . [T]he focus was small, and true, and it seemed like an effective technique to help one person at a time. And I could get my head around that.[43]

Harrison resonated with the purpose and intent of Urgent Action: protection for individuals and, if at all possible, action quick enough to prevent torture from occurring. He describes his work in a direct, unpretentious way, and often notes that "I was not the only one." But he took great satisfaction in the ultimate purpose of the work and in the mechanics of making it effective. He was also spectacularly good at it.

Designing the USA Network

Harrison first needed to build what he called "a constituency" for the Urgent Action work. Amnesty International's main connection with its members was through groups, and so groups were an obvious constituency for action on the Urgent Actions. However, local groups were organized around and devoted to support for prisoner adoption, which was a long-term process and usually served as the central focus for group participants. The logic of action was similar but, according to Harrison, if a group already was working for one or more adopted prisoners, Urgent Actions might be seen as secondary to the main work of the group. If a group put Urgent Actions on the back burner, it would

[42] Ibid.   [43] Harrison, July 17, 2013.

diminish the advantage of issuing an Urgent Action in the first place. The steady pace that groups were accustomed to when working on a long-term case was important and useful, because human rights abuses like torture can go on for a long time, said Harrison, but "to nip torture in the bud, you want to get to it right away." One obstacle to fast action was that groups usually met only once a month. He explained,

> [A]dopted prisoners were the focus of this monthly meeting. And then anything else was secondary. Including the Urgent Action alert. That doesn't mean they were disinterested, but it just means they really weren't put together for that. So, for some time, I would be sending cases out to a group contact, who would then have their network [for distribution of UAs between meetings], but we're talking about postal mail, you know, or, take the case over to your neighbor, if it's a neighborhood group. Still, it's pretty slow. It's not as slow as the third Thursday of the month, but still, not right.[44]

Adoption groups had no system in place for immediate action, although Moore noted that, pretty quickly, local group members who were asked to work on Urgent Actions caught on to the idea that "an emergency qualified as a reason for a speedy response." In addition, there were many technically savvy AI members around San Francisco in those days who were eager to find ways to work with more alacrity.

One of Moore's early duties as an office volunteer had been to meet with groups in the area to develop skilled and effective local prisoner-of-conscience adoption groups, since even those were fairly new to the West Coast. The Urgent Action process had a different dynamic and complemented prisoner adoption work:

> An Urgent Action could be a real rush for those days, for the early '70s. It would be quick. It would be a week old at the worst, or a day old.[45]

[44] Ibid. [45] Moore, July 17, 2013.

According to Moore, once the Urgent Action technique was available,

> What we needed and we did a lot of was going, first of all, to the local groups . . . In fact, I think we wound up contacting all groups both in gross mailings or calling, first groups we knew, and then groups we'd heard of.[46]

In the 1970s, Amnesty International USA's sole membership model was group membership. Group meetings were one of the first resources Harrison mined as he developed a mailing list of individuals willing to write for the Urgent Action network. Harrison sometimes used the term "case sheet," a legacy of the information sheets groups received on an adopted prisoner, to refer to the UA alerts. At the meetings that he visited around San Francisco, he would ask,

> you know, "Would you be willing to get these case sheets in the mail when they come out?" And my promise was to say, . . . "I'll only contact you when this person really needs your help, at the frequency that you want." So that's what I would promise, and you would promise to write a letter.[47]

Harrison developed a system for keeping track of how many Urgent Actions each person in the network said they could handle per month, so that the frequency of UA requests was tailored to each recipient. He also visited religious groups with other staffers or volunteers from the office who were then focusing on building interreligious constituencies for AI. These religious groups often had some sort of social action committee that might meet weekly at the social hour before or after services to work on Urgent Actions.

> There would be somebody there who would . . . copy the case sheets and have a petition, sometimes, or prewritten letters, so when people were having coffee, then, it's over on the social action table.[48]

[46] Ibid. [47] Harrison, July 17, 2013. [48] Ibid.

That mode was only weekly, Harrison emphasized, and so it was not as fast as it could be. On the other hand, sending an Urgent Action out to a group contact got more "bang for the buck," since Harrison could mail out one Urgent Action and generate several letters or a petition. He began to use a similar model informally with high school and college groups. By the late 1970s, Harrison recalled, an AI colleague named Craig Rock had developed a national network of AI campus groups that worked only on Urgent Action cases.

Harrison extended the campus-network model by involving professional associations in the Urgent Action network. Contacts in professional groups – labor unionists, teachers, doctors, psychiatrists and psychologists, other health professionals, lawyers, and people in scientific and scholarly associations, for example – could be matched with appropriate Urgent Action cases. The networks-within-network model not only generated more Urgent Actions on a case but also matched the cases with people who would identify with and commit to action on behalf of colleagues under threat. Cases involving psychiatric abuses in the Soviet Union, for example, could be sent to a volunteer in the American Psychiatric Association, who would share it with interested people in the broader membership. Other organizations might place Harrison's contact information in their professional newsletters so that members could join the Urgent Action network independently. If someone wanted only Spanish-speaking countries, or if a French class wanted to write Urgent Actions in French, that was accommodated.

The Urgent Action network was being built through AI groups, interested individuals, and people with special interests. To distribute the Urgent Actions efficiently, Harrison kept "big grids" on poster board. He divided individual participants into subgroups, sorted by how many Urgent Actions they chose to receive per month when they joined the network. Urgent Actions were mailed to segments of the network over the course of a month.

I subdivided the network in ever-increasing numbers as we got
Urgent Actions. I'd split it up so I'd have somebody to work on a case
on the 31st of the month as well as the first of the month. So I wouldn't
use everybody at the first of the month, or in the first week.[49]

Each collection of participants had a number, which enabled Harrison
to keep track of who worked on which Urgent Actions. Some were
profession- or topic-specific groups, but most groups contained individuals put together at random based on how many Urgent Actions
they promised to act on. He could assign a "little section of the network
each time I had a case."

To ensure that Urgent Actions generated at least a few nearly
immediate responses, Harrison designed a "whole other subsystem" called
a telegram tree, which Moore worked on as well. Funds for telegrams,
which were costly, were solicited through a pledge program. Members
could pledge to pay for telegrams to be composed by volunteers in the
office and sent out on the day that the Urgent Actions came in from
London.

We spent that money in little bits each day . . . [W]e would write the
messages . . . but they were all individually worded. Never two the same.
And different names. And then we would take that grid, it would be like
a template, a written template before computers, and then we would
type it out and then somebody, and it was me a lot, and Ellen a lot,
would take it down to Market Street to the Western Union office.[50]

The entire distribution system could be scaled easily as participants entered or exited the Urgent Action network. Harrison's best
guess was that a simple majority of recipients likely took action on any
given Urgent Action. Members were contacted on a regular basis with

[49] Ibid.
[50] Ibid. The telegram tree became Amnesty International USA's First Appeal Pledge
Program, which operated well into the 1990s.

a questionnaire about their participation. Those who failed to respond were dropped from the network.

> Those were painful times, because we would not hear back from hundreds of people, but we kept ourselves sort of lean and mean that way.

The system "used everybody who was willing to be used, exactly how they wanted to be used, to the benefit of the prisoners."[51]

The technique was easily adapted as improvements and new equipment became available. In 1981 or 1982, the San Francisco office acquired a computer, the first in any AI office.[52] Harrison described it as a "cube computer" in a wooden cabinet, with "big motherboards," a monitor that sat on top of the cabinet, and "a big printer." It had a modem-like appliance called a "chatbox" that could receive the UA telexes from London and convert them into digital format. Urgent Actions could then be printed to a mimeograph stencil, which was a leap forward in the mechanics of getting them out of the door to network participants.

Working from home is not unusual now, but the computer enabled a second innovation for Harrison and Moore in the early 1980s: moving the Urgent Action network to a home office. Amnesty International USA was growing as an organization, its budget was growing, and the Urgent Action network was only getting busier. At the same time, Harrison said, "Ellen and I were getting priced out of San Francisco." Harrison recognized that with a linked computer, it was possible to do the Urgent Action work "anywhere there was a phone line."

The strongest argument for a home office arrangement was the ability to staff the telex outside of office hours. As it was, when the San Francisco office opened in the morning, the London office was closing. This was convenient because the day's work for the Amnesty

[51] Ibid. [52] Ibid.

International USA network would be waiting there at the beginning of the workday. For the people at risk who were the subjects of the Urgent Actions, every hour could be precious. Working from home could be even more effective.

By the early 1980s, the Amnesty International USA headquarters was firmly established in New York, with Chicago and San Francisco designated as regional offices. Harrison broached the idea of moving the Urgent Action network hub to a home office at another Western location, where he and Moore could coordinate the network from home. He received approval from his boss, then Executive Director of Amnesty International USA Jack Healey, to look into a move.

> [B]y then, I said, look, I'm willing to do this 24/7. I don't mean staying up 24/7, but I'm willing to be on call . . . if London can get information.

Personal computers were becoming more widely available as they were considering the move. Harrison had already been convening a group of computer users in San Francisco, early Silicon Valley types, to think about how the technology could be used in AI work. Getting more of the network tasks "wired" meant it was actually thinkable to issue a graduated network response to Urgent Actions immediately, with initial responses coming within hours.

> Some researcher could get a call in the middle of the London night, they could just type on their notebook computer or their personal computer [after speaking on the] phone with their connection in Morocco, and then they could send it out to a few Urgent Action offices like me, who would get a call . . . early in the morning or late at night, whatever my time was.[53]

---

[53] Ibid.

The office already had, "basically, an emergency number." Now the Urgent Action network could be "constantly on call."

Harrison began doing the research necessary to figure out where he could establish a home office that would enable the Urgent Action network to be equally efficient, or more so. He settled on the small mountain town of Nederland, Colorado, northwest of Denver. Nederland was as far to the west of Denver as he could get, guided by two preconditions related to postal mail service, which the network still depended on for most of its distribution:

> I wanted the mail to be picked up as late as possible in the day so that I'd have time to get all the stuff done. Stuff mimeographed, put in envelopes, addressed, all that. But [the post office needed to be able to get it] sorted and flying out from the Denver airport in all directions that night.[54]

Harrison visited the main Denver post office and "looked at all these route maps," asking the postal officials, "How late can I give it to you, how early can you send it out, how far West in the mountains can I be?" And Nederland was one of "a little string of the few cities" that met Harrison's timing criteria for postal mail. In addition, it was cheap. So Harrison and Moore bought some land and built a house that included an office designed especially for the Urgent Action network on the ground floor.

They made the move in 1983, living and working in a rental until the house was finished. Like the boat, Harrison built it himself. The move "was one of the big steps of becoming more responsive and preventing torture rather than protesting the torture that had happened yesterday or last week." From the home office, they could send Urgent Actions more quickly while also sending a few telegrams as soon as they received notice from London. Harrison was confident that the earliest

[54] Ibid.

appeals mattered a lot in many cases, because immediate messages made the responsible officials "realize people know" about the abuses.

As Amnesty International USA grew, it was better able to support the Urgent Action work with resources and staffing. Amnesty International USA's Urgent Action network became the largest of any AI section. Harrison sometimes visited or provided advice to staff of some of AI's other national Urgent Action networks.[55] Moore, who already worked "shoulder to shoulder" with Harrison on Urgent Actions, came on staff after they moved to Nederland. She oversaw the telegram tree, and continued to collaborate with colleagues on human rights education, something she had started in San Francisco. She developed an "AI Kids" curriculum with spin-offs of Urgent Actions for kids, which featured a young person, along with teaching materials for instructors.[56]

In Nederland, Moore and Harrison developed a large network of volunteers that included locals from Nederland and nearby Boulder, retirees, and student interns. Amnesty International student group members from the University of Colorado Boulder would sometimes take the bus up to the house in the mountains to volunteer for an afternoon. The office usually had at least one additional paid assistant, and there were experienced local people able to step in when Moore and Harrison needed time off.

> We had long-term volunteers who were wonderful. They got out of it, all the things that we got in our early days, belongingness . . . We did get vacations because we had all these competent people.[57]

Moore also set up more formal internships for students from the University of Colorado Boulder.

The house was big, and it anchored a community network of its own in service of the Urgent Action network. At the busiest times,

---

[55] Ibid. [56] Moore, July 17, 2013. [57] Ibid.

Moore "would make a big pot of soup and then anybody who was volunteering could come up to the kitchen." Their two children, Max and Colleen, were part of the mix: "It brought all these people into their lives." Harrison also built himself a private workshop away from the fray. He found solitude doing woodcarving at the end of the day. "He was carving every day," said Moore. "No one ever went into his workshop without his inviting them in. He had that complete isolation if he needed it."[58]

Harrison and Moore coordinated Amnesty International USA's Urgent Action network out of Nederland until 2006. Asked what kept him going over all of those years in a field where burnout is so common, Harrison emphasized that his closeness to the work over decades was never a sacrifice. He said he did not burn out. Much of it was "rote," in a way, something that needed to be done over and over. Harrison did not mind that. Moore said something similar: "The repetition of the Urgent Actions was kind of a Zen thing" that grounded her other human rights work. For Harrison, the routine might be tiring, but it suited him. Getting up in the middle of the night was of no consequence. He could send something out and go "right back to bed." For Harrison, "I couldn't think of a more useful thing that I could do." Nothing was "as powerful, as productive," as the Urgent Action network. "So even though it was tiring, you know, I kept making it better so it wasn't tiring."

Harrison, who described himself as optimist, also characterized himself as a realist. The Urgent Action might not be effective every time, but with determination it could be as effective as he could make it.

> So, for 32 years. That's what we did, and . . . I just had no doubt that –
> not that it was by any stretch of the imagination 100% successful, the

---

[58] Some of Harrison's woodcarving became part of a carousel he restored with new, hand-carved animals. For images, see the website of the Carousel of Happiness, Nederland, CO (www.carouselofhappiness.org). Quotes in this paragraph are from Moore, July 17, 2013.

technique. But it was successful. In many, many cases . . . [T]o even have a hand in helping somebody, somewhere. That's successful. Just one person.[59]

Harrison used the analogy of walking down the street and seeing a stranger about to suffer violence at someone else's hands. Helping someone in that situation just once in a lifetime would be something you would always remember, he said. "I got to do that every day."

Urgent Action in Germany

Although Amnesty International USA was not one of the largest AI national sections in the early 1970s, it was an early adopter of the Urgent Action technique. Not every national branch of AI participated right away, and not every section received every Urgent Action. Even today, the Urgent Action network is something that the national sections of AI participate in to varying degrees, by choice.

The German section of AI was another of AI's largest national sections, and it became a regular participant in the permanent network. The nascent network in Germany faced a number of hurdles. Translation from English to German was one of them.[60] Staffing was another. The German section did not have a dedicated staff member until 1987, when Klaus Walter, the first Urgent Action coordinator in Germany, took on this task.[61] As a student studying law, Walter had joined a local AI group in 1976. Amnesty International appealed to him

---

[59] Harrison, July 17, 2013.

[60] Amnesty International's International Secretariat translates Urgent Actions into French and Spanish only. As of 2013, the German section shared its translations with the Austrian and Swiss sections. (Markus Bekko, interviewed by Ann Marie Clark, Bochum, Germany, May 19, 2013. At the time of the interview, Bekko was Head of the Campaigns and Communications Cluster for Amnesty International Deutschland.)

[61] Klaus Walter, interviewed by Ann Marie Clark, Bochum, Germany, May 19, 2013. Quotes in the following paragraphs are drawn from this interview.

because he was frustrated with the usual party politics in the German context. Like Harrison, he wanted to do something "useful," above all.

> I was looking for something useful to do, but sitting between all chairs, meaning not being hard-left, not being [on the] right.
> I considered myself to be a leftist, but without any affiliation to special politics. So I found Amnesty.

In 1984, Walter was hired for a national staff position – not lawyering, but editing. In 1987, he began managing the Urgent Action network. He continued until 1991, when he became Deputy Director of the German section.[62] Before 1987, the Urgent Action network was staffed mainly by conscientious objectors to Germany's mandatory military service. In those days, conscientious objectors were assigned to various forms of alternative service, including the AI office, for periods of six to eight months. That was not enough time for most of them to become skilled at the work, nor was the Urgent Action network structure very well organized, according to Walter.

Then German law changed, so that conscientious objectors could no longer be assigned to office work. "Suddenly, we [staff] had to do this, and who can do it? Okay, I can try," Walter said. In his existing portfolio, he was already proofreading the translated Urgent Actions. When the German section created two new Urgent Action staff positions, Walter took one, and a professional translator who had just finished her university studies was hired as well. Translation "is 60% of the work," said Walter. "And we began to work, not only translating every Urgent Action but also professionalizing the distribution system."

Walter explained that the German section was organized by districts, with a volunteer Urgent Action "distributor" for each district.

---

[62] Walter eventually served as Director General for Amnesty International Deutschland, beginning in 1998.

"So it was not just the staff, it was the volunteers" who did the work. Walter and a colleague organized regular meetings for the distributors and standardized the German UA format. Before, office workers had been typing the translated Urgent Actions. To simplify reproduction and mailing, they would squeeze in as many words as possible to fit on one sheet of paper, without a logo or standard format. The German section also created something like the Amnesty International USA telegram tree, responding to suggestions from the International Secretariat to recruit sponsors for telexed messages, "which were quite expensive at the time."

Although the Urgent Actions were issued by AI's International Secretariat in London, different sections could tailor their approaches. Walter's office encouraged people who might have access to a company telex machine at work, even "a normal metal firm, or whatever," to ask for permission to write a telex per month, for example. "And, it worked."

> In order for [a] secretary to be able to do that, [you had] to give them hints and a way to do it rapidly without interrupting the normal [work flow] too much.

And, he added, working with people in firms in this way was "very good experience for us," as they then began to recruit members of the West German Bundestag, the national parliament, for the Urgent Action network. They recruited state-level representatives as well. At the peak, he said, 30 percent of all Bundestag members were participating in the Urgent Action scheme, from all parties, left and right.

> [W]e had conservative people even from the right-wing party. And we tried *not* to give them only Soviet Union cases, cases they would be able to use in their own political program. Of course, we sometimes gave them a case on Cuba, but the next case would be Guatemala or from whatever, . . . keeping the balance also for them.

He noted that it would not be difficult to recruit one elected official to do a press release or write a letter on a single issue, but it was more impressive that some parliamentarians were writing letters in response to Urgent Actions once or more per month.

Walter and his colleague recruited the parliamentarians through word of mouth.

> You have to have one [member] as a good example. One was an Amnesty board member. And his secretary was an active member . . . So they were used as examples, a pattern. And the best method of recruitment was among *them*. So, if he asked his colleague, and he secretary asked her colleague then it might work. And then when they tell us, "hey, my colleague was interested," then you [had] to be quick in delivering information and showing how it works.

If all of this went well, "they would do it," said Walter. "And they really did because we [saw that] they got responses from the embassies and the governments, more than just a regular person who would write." Amazingly, according to Walter, "maybe 15–20% of them are still doing it. So this program has been going for more than 20 years."

The Urgent Action Program Now

Current national Urgent Action networks incorporate text messaging and other rapid response techniques. The digital sphere seems to be a good fit for AI activism.[63] Many AI members still use mail to send Urgent Actions, but this set of members skews toward older age groups.[64] Letter writing is

---

[63] For an analysis of issues that global NGOs face in digital advocacy, see Hans Peter Schmitz, Michael Dedmon, Tosca Bruno-van Vijfeijken, and Jaclyn Mahoney, "Democratizing Advocacy?: How Digital Tools Shape International Non-governmental Activism," *Journal of Information Technology & Politics* 17, no. 2 (2020): 174–191.

[64] Bekko, May 19, 2013.

no longer a part of daily life for many people. That likely makes the relative threshold for taking action via a traditional Urgent Action higher than it once was; digital techniques could lower the threshold. And, digital techniques are faster. Since 2012, Amnesty International UK, for example, has supplemented its traditional Urgent Actions with a text method called "Pocket Protest."[65] The pocket version adapts selected AI issues, including some UA cases, for SMS (text) communication with subscribers. Although it does not substitute for Urgent Actions, staffers see it as a way to raise the profile of Urgent Action concerns beyond existing participants.[66]

But one question regarding digital forms of participation is the relative impact. In the long view, as Moore noted,

> So what has happened with Amnesty and the UAs is we, of course, began with paper, which encouraged letters or postcards, and the telegram tree ... and then technology took over. [At first,] we were mailing the UAs to people, and they were mailing letters to officials, and then we did it both mailing and e-mailing. In the early days, when we tried to email government officials, they were changing their email addresses as fast as they could go, and so we had no idea. It's again back to the issue of effectiveness ... [W]hat do you do when the target of your appeal is able to fancy-dance and really miss getting bombarded by a lot of appeals?[67]

She added that, although current Urgent Actions offer a number of ways to contact officials, in the old days, the physical quantities of letters were thought to have an impact. That physical trace, which AI has

---

[65] Amnesty International UK, "Pocket Protest" (2021), www.amnesty.org.uk/issues/pocket-protest.

[66] Sara Rydkvist and Karen Middleton, interviewed by Ann Marie Clark, London, May 15, 2013. At the time of the interview, Rydkvist was Amnesty International UK's Urgent Action Coordinator and Middleton managed Amnesty International UK's Individuals at Risk program.

[67] Moore, July 17, 2013.

historically worked to generate as a tangible manifestation of global concern for individuals, is diminished or missing from digital approaches. In other words, according to Moore,

> Now, we really don't have an official saying, "My email box got so filled up, it crashed the system, and so I'm going to let this person go." Or, "I learned of 50,000 names on a petition."[68]

It is certainly the case that most of us alive today, including human rights violators, have little choice but to live in a digital context. Current AI campaign staff who are involved with Urgent Actions cast digital participation as one among several possible forms of multilevel activism, and as a way to generate the interest and commitment of new participants.[69]

As of 2018, Urgent Actions had not fully been adapted to digital applications. As Harrison noted, the availability of information about what is happening is unquestionably heightened by technology, and that information is easily available to more people, more quickly. Some sections, such as the USA, have implemented a template for Urgent Action that is easier to work with digitally than a PDF document, which has been the medium through which Urgent Actions are posted.[70] Sauro Scarpelli, the Deputy Director of the Campaigns Program at the International Secretariat, was careful to say that it is the action that matters, not the volume of retweets that might ricochet around the twitterverse. He noted in 2018 that AI was seeing "a lot of tweets" that simply tweeted out a URL link to the Urgent Actions on AI's website. "That doesn't help anybody. That's not an action. You need to write it and send it."[71]

---

[68] Ibid. [69] Bekko, May 19, 2013; Rydkvist and Middleton, May 15, 2013.
[70] Sauro Scarpelli, interviewed by Ann Marie Clark, London, January 17, 2018.
[71] Ibid.

Urgent Action alerts today are issued electronically. The Individuals at Risk team at the International Secretariat chooses the cases, which are issued to AI supporters through the various national sections of AI, but all sections use a similar format. The layout, although it appears in a web-friendly format, is remarkably similar to the original Urgent Actions. After a headline and a short statement of AI's concerns, each bulletin now provides a sample message in each Urgent Action with one or more addresses. Participants can click through to access a version for download, and they now have more options for communicating with government officials. Current Urgent Actions advise participants:

> Write a letter in your own words or using the sample below as a guide to one or both government officials listed. You can also email, fax, call or Tweet them.[72]

A page of background information follows the sample letter. Online, AI also asks participants to report their action back to AI, providing a link in the web-based Urgent Action and noting that "it's important to report because we share the total number with the officials we are trying to persuade and the people we are trying to help."[73]

Urgent Action as Transnational Helping Behavior

Like the prisoner adoption work for which AI first became known, the UA approach was an innovation that enabled concrete forms of transnational helping behavior for people in emergency situations. This approach is characteristic of the justice of neighborhood. Although the Urgent Action process is episodic, rather than aiming for structural

---

[72] Amnesty International USA, "Urgent Action: Disappeared during Covid-19 Quarantine (Argentina UA 120/20)" (2020), www.amnestyusa.org/urgent-actions/urgent-action-disappeared-during-covid-19-quarantine-argentina-ua-120-20/.
[73] Ibid.

change, it represents more than just a palliative approach. As Scott Harrison conceived of Urgent Action, the faster he could work to marshal AI members to write appeals, the more suffering of specific people could be stopped or prevented.

The time it takes a volunteer to read and respond to an Urgent Action alert may be relatively limited, but participation in such activity, especially repeated participation, likely builds and consolidates a number of different social ties and capacities related to justice-seeking. In a study of "courageous resistance" by "ordinary people," Thalhammer and her coauthors argue that "when people choose courageous resistance, they change the environment."[74] Their actions "define what is happening as unjust, thereby redefining the situation for others." Active dissent, "by criticizing or trying to counteract the actions of perpetrators offers hope or refuge to victims." Dissent or questioning also undermines "perpetrators' monopoly on the 'facts,' offering an interpretation that may bring even some perpetrators to question their own actions."[75] By challenging the actions of perpetrators and calling for human rights in specific cases, the Urgent Action process prompts numerous microscopic forms of altruistic action in resistance to human rights violations, empowering people to act in a way consistent with the justice of neighborhood.

Thalhammer and her coauthors suggest that, when someone has acted for others against injustice, that person becomes more committed and is "more likely to take other such actions."[76] Similarly, Daniel Carpenter and Colin Moore have found that involvement in petitioning, a less risky form of political organizing and persuasion, has legacy effects on individuals' later propensity to engage in advocacy for causes that they care about.[77] Thus, a side effect of the Urgent Action process may be that, in appealing for human rights in specific circumstances, people increase their capacity to act.

[74] Thalhammer et al., *Courageous Resistance*, 39. [75] Ibid., 39. [76] Ibid., 25.
[77] Carpenter and Moore, "When Canvassers Became Activists."

Effects and Effectiveness

As forms of appeal, Urgent Actions – and other parts of human rights practice – have many kinds of effects. They are acts of solidarity. They educate participants. They expose and oppose the most baldly violent forms of politics as carried out against individuals. As I argue in Chapter 5, they frame political acts in the language of human rights by using the language of concern and law. Having said all that, their goal is to secure safety and protection for individuals who are the persons affected by bald politics. Therefore, we all want to know whether Urgent Action works.

Urgent Actions call for a variety of remedies: access to a lawyer, medical treatment for a detainee, or release from detention. Amnesty International's published estimates for whether Urgent Actions make a "positive difference" in a case have ranged as high as 30–40 percent. For example, a 2014 report estimated that one-third of UA cases saw a positive difference.[78] In addition, it may be impossible to tell what an Urgent Action may have prevented from occurring. When asked in 2018, Sauro Scarpelli said AI currently calculated that 15–20 percent of Urgent Actions close with a success each year, where success is measured as a documented, positive outcome related to the purpose of the Urgent Action.[79] Standing by that more conservative figure, he added that success statistics do not consider the intangible emotional or moral support that Urgent Actions provide.

> We don't have a way to measure that. If you did, I'm sure the level would be [higher] because, since I've been doing this work, the comments that we receive . . . they say how important it was for them to receive that postcard with a message, or letter, or whatever.[80]

---

[78] Amnesty International, "Amnesty International Impact Report, 2012–2013," Amnesty International Secretariat, AI Index no. ORG 30/009/201 (October 2014), www.amnesty.org/download/Documents/8000/org300092014en.pdf.
[79] Scarpelli, January 17, 2018. [80] Ibid.

For a long time, AI refused to claim public credit for the impact of its work for individuals, acknowledging that there was no way to know for sure when a result was caused by AI's actions. This may be truer than ever. When Urgent Actions began, it was unusual to find out about torture in hidden corners of the world in real time, according to Scott Harrison, and governments were better able to hide abuses. Amnesty International was a lone voice in those early times. Nowadays, however, the media, cell phones, and even official surveillance cameras can bring nearly immediate attention to human rights abuses. In Harrison's estimation, from a perspective three decades removed from the initiation of the Urgent Action network, "definitely I'm not saying there isn't a need, but there's a little bit less of a need [for] the Urgent Action network to open people's eyes" in the first place. "Their eyes are open," and the technical side of exposing and documenting human rights abuses is far ahead of what it was when Urgent Actions began.[81] Urgent Actions may no longer be the only voices.

From a social science perspective, for all of these reasons, to establish a causal estimate of Urgent Actions' average impact under varying conditions would be complex. It is complex, too, for AI staffers. Amnesty International members themselves want to see evidence of impact, as an internal 2016 survey showed.[82] Amnesty International's website includes an "Amnesty Decoders" platform to solicit the help of volunteers in analyzing UA data and other human rights data.[83]

---

[81] Harrison, July 17, 2013.

[82] Amnesty International, "Review of the Urgent Action Campaigning Tool: Report of the Surveys to Sections and IS Staff," Amnesty International Secretariat, AI index no: ACT 60/5668/2017 (internal) (February 2017). Typescript, in possession of the author.

[83] See, for example, Amnesty International, "Urgent Actions Visualised," Amnesty International, International Secretariat (2021), https://decoders.amnesty.org/pro jects/decode-urgent-actions/results.

In a 2013 academic study, Cullen Hendrix and Wendy Wong found that Urgent Actions, as well as AI press releases, were associated with a small but positive marginal effect on the annual human rights score of autocratic governments, but yearly data on countries' human rights performance are probably not fine-grained enough to yield a fully satisfying statistical assessment of Urgent Action's effectiveness.[84]

Conclusion

The basic formula for Urgent Action has hardly changed since its inception, and the technique has been copied widely by other organizations. The long-standing technique is valued by AI staff and membership worldwide because it is simple, has a quick turnaround, and makes it possible to mobilize for human rights across international borders.[85]

The people who invented and developed the Urgent Action network were practical and problem-oriented people. Amnesty International already had a mobilizing tool – organized, individualized, letter writing – that could be used to get prisoners of conscience released. Could something like it not be adapted to protect any detainee, or potential detainee, from torture? That logic, and the pressure that came from expanding knowledge of how human rights were being

[84] Cullen S. Hendrix and Wendy H. Wong, "When Is the Pen Truly Mighty? Regime Type and the Efficacy of Naming and Shaming in Curbing Human Rights Abuses," *British Journal of Political Science* 43, no. 3 (2013): 651–672. On human rights and data issues, see also Ann Marie Clark and Kathryn Sikkink, "Information Effects and Human Rights Data: Is the Good News About Increased Human Rights Information Bad News for Human Rights Measures?" *Human Rights Quarterly* 35, no. 3 (2013): 539–568; Ann Marie Clark and Bi Zhao, "'Who Did What for Whom?' Amnesty International's Urgent Actions as Activist-Generated Data," *Journal of Human Rights* 19, no. 1 (2020): 46–66.

[85] Amnesty International, "Review of the Urgent Action Campaigning Tool."

violated, pushed AI to use its mobilizing tool in a new way and for a new purpose.

Owning an effective tool that *can* reduce suffering creates a corresponding obligation to use that tool justly, to maintain it well, and to see if it can be improved. That entailed hard-headed realism as well as steadfastness. For Ulltveit-Moe, it meant having a substantive response for people like the early-1970s' Brazilian expats in Germany, who emphasized that adoption was not going to work in their sorts of situations. For Harrison, it meant choosing work that he thought would be effective, and remaining clear-eyed about how to keep the network streamlined and efficient: "I believed in this network and I didn't want to screw around with pretending things were being done when they weren't."[86] The work also required steadfastness of staff and partici-pants, because although there was strong pressure to act quickly, information about results was not always forthcoming.

For Tracy Ulltveit-Moe and Scott Harrison, a practical approach to human rights emergency was inspired by witnessing injus-tice, by concern about the persons affected by injustice, and by access to particular knowledge, skills, and tools that they could use to enlist others in building more justice. In coming to AI as staffers in the early 1970s, they knew what could happen to people in harm's way because of government repression. Ulltveit-Moe, with a scholarly back-ground in Latin American politics, understood the full political and human implications of what was happening in Brazil when she came to work for the international headquarters of AI in 1971. Contacts with Brazilians pressing AI to fully grasp the implications of Brazilian torture helped to drive that home. Harrison's practical war experience as an enlisted US Marine in Vietnam and later, as a veteran returning to a very different USA, had instilled in him a suspicion of the capabilities of large systems. However, he felt an impetus to use his organizational

[86] Harrison, July 17, 2013.

skills to build the quickest, most practical, small-scale "system" possible at the time to disseminate appeals intended to block torture and other forms of repression as they were happening.

Human rights practices, as we can see through the example of Urgent Action, become tools in work for justice through repetition and refinement. The Urgent Action technique exhibited several features of what it means to build global justice: defining political repression as acts of injustice against individuals; creating the knowledge and capacity to allow others to take action for people in a global neighborhood; responding to emergency in the neighborhood; and standing up against power through words and action.

5

A Human Rights Culture of Argument

The Language of Care and Law in Urgent Action Appeals

To assist people in harm's way from current or imminent human rights violations, nongovernmental organizations (NGOs) and individuals can draw on available information and match that with rhetorical resources as they call for protection of individuals and changes in state behavior. The more that is known about global human rights violations, however, the more urgency presents itself. As a result of challenges to its original methods, in the 1970s, Amnesty International (AI) expanded its organizational mandate to oppose torture and other forms of severe and life-threatening treatment of individuals by government authorities. Amnesty International's trailblazing appeals technique, Urgent Action (UA), was an innovation to address these human rights threats. This chapter explores the contents of the thousands of UA bulletins from 1975 through 2007. By analyzing references to law and aspects of justice in the thousands of Urgent Actions, we can observe change and continuity in human rights appeals by AI over many years.

Because the UA approach has been used for so long, each individual bulletin can now be viewed as part of a series. The series comprises an unparalleled record of individuals under human rights threat across many years and many countries. Each Urgent Action represents a person or set of individuals for whom a community of concerned human rights advocates has intervened across national borders. The bulletin series is more than that, however. As a set of records of a distinct advocacy technique, the texts can be plumbed for patterns and changes in this prominent approach to justice-seeking.

Urgent Actions have proved flexible and adaptable as a form of advocacy. Elements of the justice of neighborhood and of the political realization of justice are visible in this temporal record. As described in Chapter 3, the justice of neighborhood refers to the regular expression of active care and concern, while the political realization of justice refers to the tools of law and argument that address politics more directly. Throughout the time period, the Urgent Actions give voice to the active care found in the justice of neighborhood by expressing, for example, fear for a person's safety, and by inquiring about alleged ill-treatment of people by authorities or their agents. Appeals to global human rights norms in the documents indicate the emerging importance of law as a tool for the political realization of justice at the global level.

Urgent Action Appeals and Changes in Human Rights Language

In their own right, the UA documents are significant historical records of AI's advocacy. The documents are synopses of human rights threats to specific individuals, along with requests for possible remedies, as AI identified and reported them. Aside from the factual information each record contains, the documents comprise a unique collection of discursive data: the language used to meet the urgency of transnational human rights aid is encapsulated in each bulletin. The bulletins are oriented toward protecting persons across the globe who may be threatened or taken into custody by agents of the state. Not surprisingly, then, references to various aspects of law figure in many of the appeals, although the bulletins are not legal documents. For example, an appeal might cite widely accepted legal principles such as habeas corpus, the right to know the charges against oneself, and aspects of law that AI sees as relevant to a person's situation.

As noted previously, the work of James Boyd White, a scholar of classics and law, models a potentially fruitful way to conceive of human rights language as a culture of argument. I use the concept to analyze the contents of the UA documents. The language in the Urgent Actions is conceived as a set of arguments for human rights protection, reflecting the human rights movement's use of information and legal standard-setting from the 1970s onward. What justifications does AI employ in its calls for aid to individuals facing human rights abuses? As argumentation, how does AI frame its appeals to human rights as principles of right and wrong? Do the appeals reflect the growing availability of legal norms in the international system? Do they stay close to the care expressed in the justice of neighborhood, or do they invoke specific global legal standards in the effort to protect individuals in threatening circumstances?

In White's essay, "The Dissolution of Meaning," arguments related to justice *lost* their meaning as Athens gained power and abandoned debates about justice and fairness, right and wrong.[1] In contrast, during the broad time span in which the UA texts have been produced, arguments referring to human rights have *gained* meaning in international politics. When the first UA appeals were launched in 1973, neither of the two treaties implementing the principles enumerated by the 1948 Universal Declaration on Human Rights (UDHR) was in force. The International Covenant on Civil and Political Rights and the International Covenant on Economic, Social, and Cultural Rights had been adopted in 1966, but they did not enter into force until 1976.[2] By

---

[1] White, "The Dissolution of Meaning," see especially 59, 67, 89, 89 n.41 (303).

[2] "International Covenant on Civil and Political Rights," (999 U.N.T.S. 171; S. Exec. Doc. E, 95–2 (1978); S. Treaty Doc. 95–20; 6 I.L.M. 368 (1967), entered into force March 23, 1976, December 16, 1966); "International Covenant on Economic, Social

the time the series analyzed here ended, in 2007, global standard-setting for the general protection of rights to physical integrity had largely been completed.

White looks for evidence of a culture of argument in the way that speech is used. To recall his approach, language shows "the discourse, the conventions of argument and action, by which [actors] maintain and regulate their relations with each other."[3] Temporal changes in how appeals are expressed are treated as arguments that the actors constructed in an effort to advance persuasive or meaningful argument in contemporaneous context.

In the Urgent Actions viewed as human rights appeals, the correspondence is one-sided. But we can still assume that the language used by human rights actors likely shapes and is shaped by historical continuities and traditions, as well as the emergence of newly recognized or newly contested issues, new law, and emerging norms – that is, standards of appropriate behavior for actors with a given identity.[4] Amnesty International has been a key speaker of this language in its work for transnational advocacy for individuals, and the Urgent Actions offer a rich field for investigating its content. The UA texts thus permit us to explore the language of human rights appeals during a critical period for human rights.

I start by assuming each bulletin to be, first, a message enlisting aid for individuals in need; second, a message enabling informed participation; and third, a strategic template for putting pressure on states to change their treatment of people within a given target state's jurisdiction. As such, we might expect the appeals to include some combination of expressions of care and concern, references to

and Cultural Rights," (993 U.N.T.S. 3; S. Exec. Doc. D, 95-2 (1978); S. Treaty Doc. No. 95-19; 6 I.L.M. 360 (1967), 1966).

[3] White, "The Dissolution of Meaning," 59.

[4] This definition of norms appears in Finnemore and Sikkink, "International Norm Dynamics and Political Change," 891.

principles of law and, possibly, calls for justice. Because these are not legal documents, legal norms might not be the first resort as a source of mobilization. If law is invoked in a sustained way by participants in grassroots efforts, however, we can view references to legal norms and principles as part of an argument that was thought to carry meaning. This would constitute evidence of law's entry into the human rights culture of argument, and therefore an increasing turn toward arguments advancing the political realization of justice.

Based on general inspection of the UA bulletins, it is apparent that some forms of law are used in the documents. What kinds of law? Do we see mention of basic domestic legal principles related to affected persons' circumstances? Are international human rights standards invoked in the document as they enter into force? Given the growth in availability of global legal norms to support human rights, do references to legal principles track with the increasing availability of law? This is by no means certain, given that the UA approach was a grassroots endeavor. Did ideas drawn from new human rights standards enter the urgent appeals and become part of the human rights culture of argument?

The first question I explore is whether references to international law and global human rights standards increase in the texts over time. In light of the proliferation of global legal norms of human rights since the 1970s, the language of the bulletins should reflect an increasingly dense human rights culture of argument, as seen in more numerous global references to these principles.[5] If global human rights

---

[5] In a note on the prevalence of human rights discourse, Geoff Dancy finds that written references to human rights between 1975 and 2010, as found in Google's digital book archive, increased steadily at a rate that tracks with the number of global human rights treaty ratifications. His observation is compatible with the idea of a developing human rights culture of argument. See Geoff Dancy, "Human Rights Pragmatism: Belief, Inquiry, and Action," *European Journal of International Relations* 22, no. 3 (2016): 519.

standards begin to appear in the texts of the Urgent Actions, when they did not appear before, then there is a stronger case to be made that we are observing a change in the human rights culture of argument. The evidence would then be consistent with the proposition that arguments rooted in common legal principles as political reasoning would be persuasive to the public and to public officials, since the bulletins had a dual role as mobilizing messages to AI constituencies and as templates for the network members to use when addressing state officials.

The second query explores the relative balance between law and indications of concern for the well-being of people at risk. If law becomes more prominent in the human rights culture of argument, does language more closely related to care and the justice of neighborhood diminish over time? In other words, we know that attention to the particular situations of persons named in the UA bulletins marked AI's earliest case-based appeals for prisoners of conscience. Is law displacing or complementing the importance of aid to the stranger in the UA approach?

The balance between forms of concern and legal justice-seeking has normative implications for human rights practice. Although a comprehensive view of justice includes concern for the lives of individuals, law introduces more explicitly political tools of justice. On the other hand, if urgent care needs to be sensitive to local conditions, are expressions of active care, part of the justice of neighborhood, weakened by increasing focus on global law? Analyzing the use of law alongside expressions of concern in the UA documents offers a way to observe the balance of such concerns. In the next section I describe the data drawn from the UA documents and discuss the strategy of inquiry.

Urgent Actions as a Form of Human Rights Appeal

The Urgent Actions report on imminent violence or threats to individuals that infringe upon the human rights of the affected persons and require immediate action to avert harm. They are brief, one to two pages each, and follow a consistent approach with three general features. First, Urgent Actions are issued for individuals, but sometimes also name sets of individuals or groups. A single Urgent Action might be issued on behalf of three union members arrested at the same time, for example. Second, the bulletins often refer to principles that are being violated by these acts. The principled reference points vary: they range from concern for the safety or well-being of persons under threat, legal rules pertaining to treatment of detainees, and national law, as well as regional or global human rights standards. Third, bulletins direct the readers (i.e., participants in AI's Urgent Action network) to compose their own appeals to named officials of the government of the affected persons. The officials' titles, names, and contact details are contained in the text of the document.

Because the Urgent Actions form a series of influence attempts related to human rights violations, their contents crucially reflect contemporary issues related to human rights in international politics. Through the Urgent Action process, actors such as state officials, NGOs and their members, intergovernmental organizations (IGOs), those who have suffered from human rights abuses, and others initiate and respond to claims before a broader audience composed of similar actors and, to some extent, the public. As in law and diplomacy, the Urgent Actions appeal for a desired action. An appeal can entail reference to principles and values that may lend added force to an argument. An appeal may also include a nod to the power, prestige, or procedural authority of the addressee or a third party. The patterns and singularities in the ways actors lodge such claims over time paint a picture of the dynamics of this particular culture of argument.

Urgent Actions as Data

The content of the texts could be explored in many ways. I focus on the texts as repeated snapshots of a form of human rights action over time.

As an advocacy technique, the bulletins need to be understood within the organizational ambitions and goals of AI. Those appeals can be expected to reveal the contemporaneous possibilities and contextual limits of advocacy. As a form of discursive action, their content and messaging can be sifted for clues to changes in normative points of reference.

Who Is Speaking? Who Is the Audience?

In analyzing the Urgent Actions as a kind of discourse, it is important to take into account the authors and the audience in the Urgent Action process, as well as the Urgent Actions' textual content and changes in that content over time.[6] Amnesty International staffers author the UA documents. The initial recipients of the Urgent Action are not the governments who are targets of the appeals but Urgent Action network participants. The UA bulletins were originally sent by mail to AI groups and individual members of the Urgent Action network, as it has been called in the USA. With the advent of UA postings on the web and social media, some people moved to participate may have only weak ties to AI as an organization. For AI and for participants in the Urgent Action process, government officials are the second, but primary, target of the appeal's content. Since participants are asked to compose their own messages, UA participants become the eventual second authors of the appeals. Table 5.1 summarizes the process.

As a form of representation, then, the UA texts have at least two constituencies. Like many NGOs working on behalf of a cause, AI publicly claims to represent a dual constituency: its members and the people it is working to protect.[7] The Urgent Actions are issued to one

---

[6] Kevin C. Dunn and Iver B. Neumann, *Undertaking Discourse Analysis for Social Research* (Ann Arbor: University of Michigan Press, 2016).

[7] Laura Montanaro explores this aspect of representation in *Who Elected Oxfam? A Democratic Defense of Self-appointed Representatives* (Cambridge: Cambridge University Press, 2018).

Table 5.1 *The Urgent Action process*

1	2	3	4	5
Information comes to AI about persons who would benefit from urgent assistance as a result of imminent rights violations, physical harm, or threats to rights	AI's International Secretariat verifies the information and issues 'Urgent Action' containing information and recommended action to national sections	AI's national offices coordinate the distribution of the action bulletin to AI members and participants (then: via postal mail; now: via email, web posting, direct messaging)	Participants write appeals to officials on behalf of the individuals named in the bulletin (then: via letter, fax, or telegram; now: via letter and electronic means)	The target country's government officials receive messages urging them to act to prevent or stop violations, and provide redress

constituency, AI's members, on behalf of a second constituency, those whose human rights are being violated. By using Urgent Actions to inform their own appeals, AI members both lodge claims on behalf of others and implicitly endorse AI's authority to make such claims.

Describing the double authorship and double appeal is no arcane exercise. Beyond their primary purpose, the Urgent Actions comprise a form of communication between AI and those who are being asked to lodge the appeals. In taking part in active care by responding to an Urgent Action, participants not only assist the affected person but they also support a tool of human rights practice that is believed to become more effective when lots of people take part.

The UA texts contain a remarkable amount of relatively technical information. This secondary authorship that they invite requires the communication of political background relevant to the affected person's situation, as well as information about legal issues and other details related to the appeal. Thus, the Urgent Actions educate participants about human rights as they ask correspondents to put the knowledge into action.

Typical Structure and Content of an Urgent Action

In this section, I describe the Urgent Actions' typical structure and content in more detail. A title features the major concern AI has about the case. The person's name and country, and sometimes the age, occupation, or other information about the affected person, are often listed below the title. The first part of the bulletin details AI's concern in a paragraph or two, offering factual information that describes the conditions, experiences, or events that pose a human rights threat to the affected person or persons. The initial detail is followed by background information. The background gives more context to AI's concern. It may describe prevailing political conditions in the country, or comment on the scope and nature of similar threats made to others, for example. The alleged perpetrators of the harm are identified, if known. In a concluding section, each Urgent Action typically lists a handful of recommended requests that participants should make of government officials. These may include expressions of concern for a detainee's medical condition, requests that officials investigate the circumstances of an apparent abduction by state agents, or demands that persons deemed to be responsible for the rights violations be held accountable by the authorities.

Over the years, AI developed variations on the Urgent Action. In addition to the Urgent Action as the basic and usual form of appeal, a smaller selection of specialized appeals could be issued based on urgency or the leverage that members of professional networks might have in appealing for a colleague. The special types of alerts have included telexes asking national UA coordinators to muster a small number of immediate responses that could be sent over the wires. Medical Actions (MAs), addressing specific medical concerns for an affected person, can be sent to a limited groups of network participants with special interest or expertise in medical care. Amnesty International also occasionally provides follow-up information to participants in later bulletins, called "Follow-ups." Follow-ups might offer new information about the status of the person named in the original appeal and ask network participants to write again about a new or continuing issue relevant to the case, to send a follow-up message acknowledging a positive action by the authorities, or to cease action altogether. All of these documents were issued as public, or what AI calls "external," documents.[8]

Data and Method

The main research questions of interest pertain to changes in the culture of argument concerning human rights and justice in the UA appeals. To get at this question, I have relied on extensive coding of the texts. This project was made more tractable because Amnesty International USA's original UA coordinator, Scott Harrison, kept a physical copy of each UA alert on file from 1975 until his retirement in 2006, when the files moved to Amnesty International USA's Washington office. With AI's formal permission, in 2013, our research team at Purdue University began digitizing the physical UA documents

---

[8] Amnesty International has sometimes issued another kind of bulletin in limited numbers, called a WARN, sent to known and trusted network members, which contained internal information not to be made public but which could be incorporated in targeted communications.

as part of a research and library preservation project. The project digitized and coded all available UA bulletins issued by AI from 1975 through 2007.[9]

NVivo software was used to identify and tag, or code, terms in each UA text. The coding scheme encompassed references to justice, law, legal standards of human rights, domestic law, descriptive characteristics of each case, and other features of the Urgent Actions. The richness and sheer size of the sample of texts necessitated quantitative tools, transparency of coding, and interpretative judgment. The coding team stuck closely in most cases to clearly defined criteria to minimize coding variation. This was feasible because the documents' format showed little variation, and particular phrases tended to recur, facilitating common coding rules. Data are based on coding of all available bulletins issued by AI's Urgent Action network from 1975 through 2007. For reasons of manageability and of resource limitations, given the time-intensive nature of the work, the current analysis was limited to the alerts in the designated thirty-three–year span.

Coders were instructed to code the documents for any appearance of the word "justice." The team coded the word "justice" only if it

---

[9] Formal permission and access for the project was granted by Amnesty International USA. Additional advice and assistance was provided by staff of AI's records unit at the International Secretariat in London. For more information, see Amy Barton, Paul Bracke, and Ann Marie Clark, "Digitization, Data Curation, and Political Science Research: The Amnesty International Urgent Action Bulletins Project," *IASSIST Quarterly* 40, no. 1 (2016): 28–35. The project was assisted by a grant from Purdue University: Ann Marie Clark and Paul Bracke, "Human Rights Texts for Digital Research: Archiving and Analyzing Amnesty International's Historic 'Urgent Action' Bulletins at Purdue University." The project was reviewed and approved by Purdue University Human Protection Program. Ref. no. 0909008498, "Transnational Human Rights Work for Individuals, 1974–2007: Amnesty International's Urgent Action Bulletins" (Ann Marie Clark, principal investigator, exemption approval date October 13, 2009 and May 9, 2013). The digital records will be made available online at Purdue University Libraries' e-Archives. Recent UAs can be found at AI's global website, www.amnesty.org.

appeared in the text, with the exception of when the specific term "rule of law" appeared, which was extremely rare. Under the general code of justice, coders chose from a selection of more specific coding categories. At the beginning of the project, the following definition was selected as a succinct basis for identifying possible aspects of justice that might appear:

> Justice is [a] complex moral concept relating to human relationships generally, but closely associated with the operation of legal institutions. Justice concerns both the correct or fair distribution of benefits and burdens as between groups or classes of persons (social justice), and treating individuals properly or fairly (individual justice). More specifically, justice can be about the proper basis for agreements or exchanges (commutative justice) or about putting right past wrongs or injustices (corrective justice). In all these spheres, justice may be focused on defining the proper outcomes of social relationships (substantive or material justice) or on the processes or procedures that ought to be followed in reaching these outcomes (formal or procedural justice). Procedures may be considered formally just insofar as they result in a substantively just outcome, but, in cases of "pure procedural justice," where the desired outcome is not known or in dispute, procedures may be considered just or unjust independent of their results, if, for instance, they are thought to be fair and impartial.[10]

Because of the known scope of issue coverage expected in the Urgent Actions, and in parallel with the theoretical discussion in the introductory chapters, the main focus of coding was expected to be in the distinction between "social justice" (or "substantive or material justice") and "formal or procedural justice."

---

[10] Tom Campbell, "Justice," in *The New Oxford Companion to Law*, eds. Peter Cane, Joanne Conaghan, and David M. Walker (Oxford: Oxford University Press, 2008).

The project also created codes for various kinds of concerns for the affected persons' immediate well-being. Invocation of such concerns did not use the word "justice" but appeared frequently as part of what the librarians affiliated with the project would characterize as terms "native" to AI. The most common of these included "fear for safety" and "legal concern." Both phrases appear over the full range of years and countries. However, we found that "legal concern" as a category was somewhat inconsistent, so it is not included in the analysis presented here. Instead, only references to particular forms of law at the global, regional, or national levels are included.

Coders identified several other specific and consistent references to law. In general, specific standards at the global or regional level were coded hierarchically. Some standards were coded individually. For example, the UDHR was coded individually, but within the coding structure, it also fell within the broader category of "law and legal standards, global." Others were grouped without individual coding. For example, because there is so much variety at the national level, domestic law or institutional provisions were coded under "national law, institutional framework, and policies." This coding category included references to specific legal measures, protections in a country's constitution or other domestic law, the national legislative framework and judicial practices, the existence of a national human rights institution, and other issues related to the national context of human rights protection.

For purposes of consistency and simplicity, only the standard Urgent Actions were included in the following analysis. Follow-ups or other specialized bulletins are excluded. Reference counts drawn from the coding were exported to statistical software for analysis. If the same term appeared repeatedly in a single document, it was counted only once. The analysis presented here includes all primary, or standard, UA documents that are in the collection, spanning from 1975 through

2007.[11] It excludes documents like Follow-ups, MAs, and other more limited forms of appeal. The bar chart in Figure 5.1 depicts the number of Urgent Actions issued yearly in this period across the globe.

Geographical Coverage

The map in Figure 5.2 illustrates the geographical distribution of the standard Urgent Actions by country.[12] Geographical distribution of the

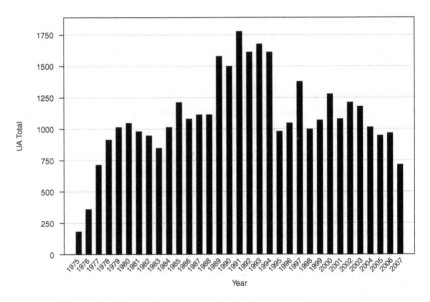

Figure 5.1 Urgent Actions, issued globally by year, 1975–2007

---

[11] The following graphs and discussion are technically considered to be based on an analysis of a "sample," since comparison with AI's master list indicated that a negligible number of the physical UAs are missing from the collection.

[12] Figure 5.2 is a reproduction of a map that originally appeared in Clark and Zhao, "'Who Did What for Whom?'" Reprinted with permission.

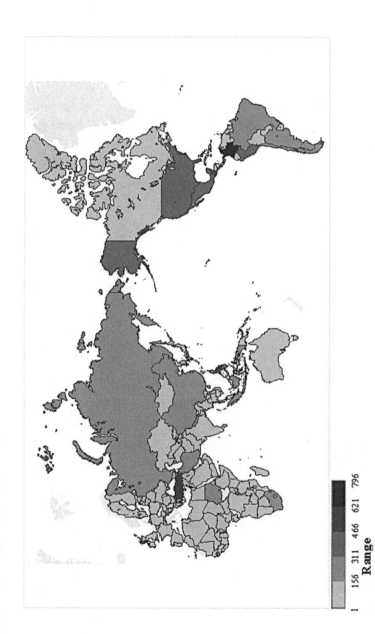

Figure 5.2 Urgent Action totals, range by country, 1975–2007

Urgent Actions was global, but the collection of UA bulletins is clearly not randomly distributed, either geographically or with regard to all human rights violations that may have occurred. At the inception of the UA technique, AI issued Urgent Actions on a global selection of countries, but not all. Amnesty International's famous *Annual Report* has become a source of record for global analysis of human rights violations, but in social science terms, the size and scope of the underlying population of human rights violations is unknown at any given time.[13]

The temporal and geographic distribution of the Urgent Actions is also to some degree dependent on information available to AI and the choices AI made concerning which cases are appropriate for UA appeals. At the outset, for example, assignment of a case as a Urgent Action was less standardized than it is now. According to Tracy Ulltveit-Moe, AI's country researchers made the main decision to request Urgent Action for cases that they worked on in the early years, and individual researchers did not adopt the technique uniformly.[14] Now, Urgent Actions are still selectively issued, but the decision is based on a set of considerations about whether the technique is appropriate for the case.[15]

Turkey and Colombia had the highest totals of Urgent Actions over the 1975–2007 period. Other Latin American countries that were subject to heavy coverage included Peru, Mexico, and Guatemala. A seeming anomaly visible on the map can be explained partly by AI's campaigning choices. The map locates the USA in a category of countries that have higher than the median cumulative number of

[13] This is a common concern with human rights data; see Clark and Sikkink, "Information Effects and Human Rights Data."

[14] Ulltveit-Moe, May 15, 2013.

[15] Leonore Rebassa, interviewed by Ann Marie Clark, London, January 18, 2018. At the time of the interview, Rebassa was Senior Campaigner, Individuals at Risk team, at AI's International Secretariat.

Urgent Actions when compared with other countries. Its totals cause the USA to fall in a higher category than Russia or China. The high US numbers are largely due to the fact that AI has long used Urgent Actions to campaign against capital punishment in the USA.

The US example illustrates why the Urgent Actions should not be seen as a direct reflection of the distribution of all human rights violations around the world, although as events data, they contain valuable information applicable to broader human rights investigations.[16] The strength of this collection is its status as a complete set of all of a certain kind of appeal as issued by a major human rights actor and, as such, it is useful as events-based data on a large set of incidents addressed by AI, including the ways that AI characterized its appeals over time.

The bar chart in Figure 5.3 depicts the total of Urgent Actions in the data set, by region.[17] Amnesty International issued the highest number of Urgent Actions on Latin America in the 1975–2007 period, as the figure makes clear. The UA approach was conceptualized with reference to torture in Latin America, as Chapter 4 explained, and threats to individuals in those countries were some of the earliest to be met with UA appeals. In addition, events in Latin America constituted key cases for the development of United Nations (UN) procedures and standard-setting on human rights, particularly concerning torture and disappearances, as well as the forging of links among global and local human rights activists.[18] For these reasons, Latin America

[16] Clark and Zhao, "Who Did What for Whom?"

[17] The chart groups countries based on the country code found in the Correlates of War (COW) data; some of these differ from AI's region designations. The COW country codes can be viewed online at https://correlatesofwar.org/data-sets/cow-country-codes/. In Figure 5.3, for example, "Europe" refers to country codes 200–395; "Middle East" refers to country codes 630–698; and "Asia" refers to country codes 700–817, encompassing Asia, South Asia, and Asia-Pacific.

[18] Iain Guest, *Behind the Disappearances* (Philadelphia: University of Pennsylvania Press, 1992); Clark, *Diplomacy of Conscience*; Keck and Sikkink, *Activists beyond Borders*.

constitutes a critical case for examining the possible development of a culture of argument related to law, justice, and on human rights. Because of their numeric frequency within the full collection of Urgent Actions, and because of AI's intensive work on Latin America during periods of serious repression, this region also offers the potential for the fullest view of change over time in Urgent Actions' appeals content. In the following section, I begin with the regional subset of Latin American UA bulletins and then compare them with the set of Urgent Actions from the rest of the world.

Results

With reference to the Urgent Actions' content, one can ask, "in what sorts of argument might they engage, making what claims or appeals, accepting what modes of reasoning?" For White, the speeches presented in Thucydides' *History* reflect change in what the parties expect of one another at given points in time.[19] I approach the language of the Urgent Actions in a similar way with regard to the kinds of arguments that are deployed in the UA cases identified by AI. In other words, if we assume that AI was making what it believed were the most persuasive arguments in light of all possible arguments available, then the terms of the argument are likely to be revealing of the culture in which human rights appeals occur – including the discursive resources available to AI in this context. The UA documents incorporate phrases, requests, and arguments that have remained relatively stable over time. However, as White points out, shifts in phrases, facts, or points of reference may reveal changes in the rhetorical

---

[19] James Boyd White, "A Way of Reading," in *When Words Lose Their Meaning: Constitutions and Reconstitutions of Language, Character, and Community* (Chicago: University of Chicago Press, 1984), 7.

resources used by the actors and, thus, possible shifts in their culture of argument.

The cumulative coding of the texts, while not heavily nuanced, creates a sketch based on empirical evidence of variation in the characterizations of justice, law, and concern in this large body of bulletins. To preview the findings discussed later, references to law do recur in the Urgent Actions as appeals, with variation in levels and content over time. However, the appeals are dominated by procedural forms of justice, if we count only explicit uses of justice. The increasing prevalence of law and procedure-related advocacy, I argue, reflects the importance of a growing legal culture – and thus an institutionalization of a human rights culture of argument – over decades. On the other hand, calls for care and well-being as part of the justice of neighborhood can be more subtle than calls for procedure. Invocation of concern for individuals' well-being, health, and safety are widespread and persistent, particularly in periods where we can infer that patterns of human rights violations were most acute. However, the UA method was not used to address broader social justice issues as economic, social, or cultural rights in this period, and therefore, the bulletins do not incorporate such rights to any significant degree. Other interesting patterns related to the meaning and pursuit of justice as articulated in the appeals also come into view.

Law in the Human Rights Culture of Argument: Latin America and Globally

The Urgent Actions show notable shifts in the nature of their references to law, as well as a marked rise in mentions of human rights standards in the documents. As strategies for addressing urgent human rights situations, these shifts seem to reflect the availability and growth of global human rights standards. Figures 5.4 and 5.5 illustrate the appearance of references to domestic law generally, to regional human rights

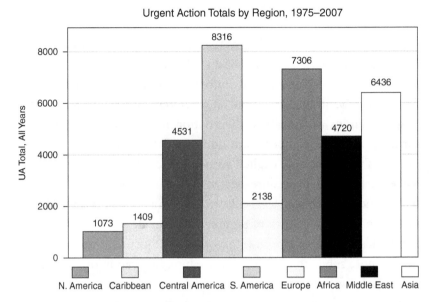

Figure 5.3 Urgent Action totals, by region, 1975–2007

standards, and to global human rights standards, in Latin America (Figure 5.4) and elsewhere (Figure 5.5). Calculated percentages of Urgent Actions are presented rather than raw counts in each of the figures in this chapter.[20]

Amnesty International's approach to advocacy within countries has long been attentive to existing domestic legal standards and institutions. In urgent situations, pressing a country to follow principles likely has more impact if the principles are already established in domestic law and policy. Domestic features of law and policy as

[20] Along with the scatterplots of each year's values in Figures 5.4–5.9, a summary line created using the Lowess procedure is also depicted for each data series. Lowess regression is a statistical technique for data visualization that estimates local weighted regressions to fit smoothed curves through scatterplots. The Lowess lines are noted by the term "fitted" in the legend of each graph.

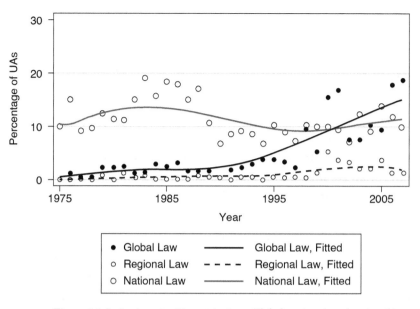

Figure 5.4 Latin America Urgent Actions: Global, regional, and national law, 1975–2007

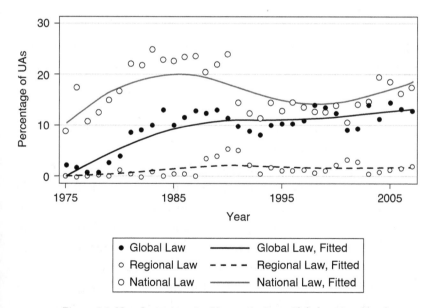

Figure 5.5 Non-Latin America Urgent Actions: Global, regional, and national law, 1975–2007

invoked in the UA documents are not all specifically human rights-related but instead tend to refer to general civil or legal protections, such as habeas corpus, or legal arrangements or decisions relating to the general circumstances of a UA case. They are sometimes assertions of legal principle on behalf of the affected person, and sometimes describe features of the person's domestic legal case. The figures show that references to national law are relatively constant across the whole period. In Latin America, some reference to domestic law (referring to national law, institutional, legal, and political framework, and policies) appeared in roughly 10–20 percent of all Urgent Actions between 1975 and 1990. This leveled off somewhat after 1990, but still held steady at or just below 10 percent. References to domestic law were slightly higher in number as of the mid-1980s, but evidenced the same pattern.

The regional and global law categories represent explicit references to regional or international human rights standards. To begin with regional law, there is little evidence of an uptick in references to regional standards in urgent cases. Even in Latin America, where regional human rights law is relatively well developed in comparison with other regions, there are very few references to regional human rights law. Until the late 1990s, the percentage of Urgent Actions invoking any regional standard is close to zero in Latin America and not much higher globally.

In contrast, the frequency of references to global human rights standards in Latin America as a percentage of Urgent Actions begins to match and then outpace references to national law by the late 1990s. The pattern supports a view that references to global law had begun to comprise a significant part of the human rights culture of argument by this time. In the late 1970s, Urgent Actions were used frequently in AI's work on Chile and Argentina, and AI's work to develop international norms was honed in response to conditions in these countries. During this early period, however, although law was being invoked in up to 15 percent of all Urgent Actions, global law mentions were close to zero. The UN Convention against Torture, for example, had not been opened for signing until 1984.[21] After 1987, when it entered into force, it is not mentioned in the Urgent Actions issued on Chile and Argentina. The global treaty most frequently referred to in the UA documents on this region prior to the 1990s is the International Covenant on Civil and Political Rights.[22] Other global legal standards mentioned by AI in the early period with regard to Latin America include declarations or nontreaty standards, such as the UDHR, for example, or, less frequently, the UN's Standard Minimum Rules for the Treatment of Prisoners.[23]

By 2007, the percentage of Urgent Actions that mention global standards exceeds that of references to domestic law and policy, reaching 20 percent in some years. A wider selection of standards was also being invoked, from the Convention against Torture to the Universal Declaration on Human Rights Defenders.[24] This differs starkly from the pattern at the beginning of the period, when global law mentions were sparse. In the rest of the world, there was also a distinct rise in the use of global law that comes close to the level of domestic law by the end of the series. Consequently, it seems safe to infer that the legal references

[21] United Nations, "Convention against Torture and Other Cruel, Inhuman or Degrading Treatment or Punishment" (G.A. res. 39/46, [annex, 39 U.N. GAOR Supp. (No. 51) at 197, U.N. Doc. A/39/51 (1984)], entered into force June 26, 1987).

[22] "International Covenant on Civil and Political Rights" (G.A. res. 2200A [XXI], 21 U.N. GAOR Supp. [No. 16] at 52, U.N. Doc. A/6316 [1966], entered into force March 23, 1976).

[23] "Universal Declaration of Human Rights" (1948); United Nations, "Standard Minimum Rules for the Treatment of Prisoners" (adopted by the First United Nations Congress on the Prevention of Crime and the Treatment of Offenders, and approved by the Economic and Social Council, res. 663 C [XXIV] of July 31, 1957 and res. 2076 [LXII] of May 13, 1977).

[24] "Declaration on the Right and Responsibility of Individuals, Groups and Organs of Society to Promote and Protect Universally Recognized Human Rights and Fundamental Freedoms" (UNGA Res. A/RES/53/144, adopted December 9, 1998 [commonly known as the UN Declaration on Human Rights Defenders]).

prevalent in the older Urgent Actions broadened to include global human rights standards as part of the human rights culture of argument. Did justice enter that argument?

Justice as Accountability and Concern in the Culture of Argument: Latin America and Globally

As depicted in Figure 5.6 (Latin America) and Figure 5.7 (the rest of the world), use of the word "justice" appears early and rises over time, especially in Latin America. References to justice are narrowly circumscribed within a particular aspect of formal or procedural justice: the demand that officials "bring those responsible [for violations] to justice," depicted as "bring to justice" in the figures. Direct invocation of any comprehensive, substantive conception of justice is almost completely absent from these documents.

Accountability as a Part of Procedural Justice

The "bring to justice" demand places the responsibility for the investigation and prosecution of human rights violations on the government officials who are the addressees. This form of appeal to justice emphasizes that some agent is responsible for a wrong that is being done, and that officials should make sure perpetrators are held accountable. Almost no other uses of the word "justice" appear, as illustrated by the overlapping lines and points in Figures 5.6 and 5.7.

The mode in which justice is invoked is remarkably stable in the documents, suggesting that AI did not change or expand the way it used explicit references to justice over time, even though it referred more frequently to bringing perpetrators to justice. These calls for accountability became more and more frequent in Latin America. The "bring to justice" phrasing occurs with dramatically greater frequency in the second half of the UA series on Latin America, with the

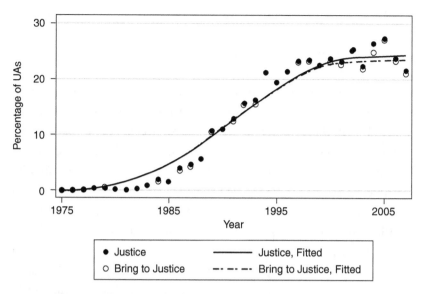

Figure 5.6 Latin America Urgent Actions: "Justice," 1975–2007

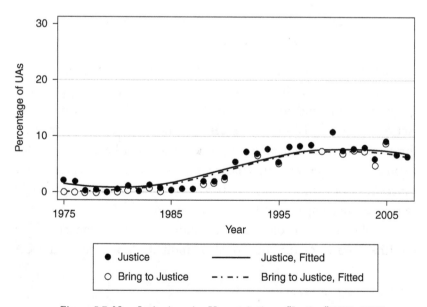

Figure 5.7 Non-Latin America Urgent Actions: "Justice," 1975–2007

usage appearing in more than one out of five (20 percent) of all Urgent Actions in Latin American Urgent Actions from the mid-1990s to the mid-2000s, as depicted in Figure 5.6.

The notable rise in Latin American Urgent Actions' requests to "bring those responsible to justice" occurs in conjunction with a period of redemocratization in many Latin American countries. This was also a period when AI was learning from the experiences of activists in that region. The relatives of victims of human rights abuses were on the leading edge of demanding accountability and condemning impunity for officials of former repressive governments.[25] The phrase "bring those responsible to justice" seems to reflect that dynamic. Justice mentions in global Urgent Actions outside of Latin America, shown in Figure 5.7, have a similar emphasis on procedural justice, but approach just under 10 percent by the end of the period, a change much smaller than the growth in such claims that is demonstrated in Latin America.

Concern as Part of the Justice of Neighborhood, and Its Co-occurrence with Accountability

As shown earlier, references to procedural justice appear frequently in the language AI uses in the documents, which would be appropriate given the short and urgently felt time frame within which Urgent Action occurs. Social justice concerns do not appear. However, pleas for safety – active indications of concern for well-being – are noted frequently and in very practical contexts. These two features, the expressions of concern and the demand that perpetrators be brought to justice, are compared in Figures 5.8 and 5.9.

References to one of AI's standard issues of concern, "fear for [the] safety" of the individual or individuals named in the UA

[25] Sikkink, *The Justice Cascade.*

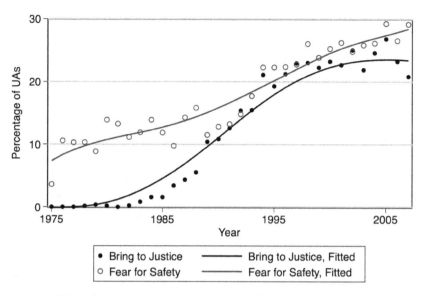

Figure 5.8 Latin America Urgent Actions: "Bring to justice" versus "fear for safety," 1975–2007

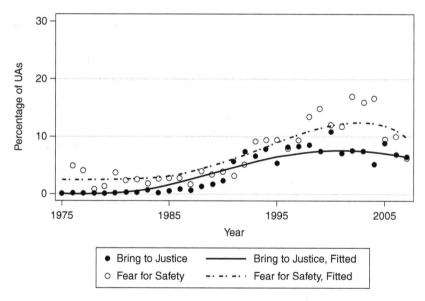

Figure 5.9 Non-Latin America Urgent Actions: "Bring to justice" versus "fear for safety," 1975–2007

bulletin, are numerous. In a typical example of how AI would use this term, a 1983 Urgent Action issued for a union worker in El Salvador notes that "it is not known whether his arrest has been officially acknowledged and there are fears for his safety."[26] The characterization of AI's concern as "fear for safety" appears in consistently rising rates in the Latin America Urgent Actions, and reaches a high of almost one in three at the end of the time under consideration. In the rest of the world, the use of "fear for safety" also increases over time, but never rises over 18 percent of all Urgent Actions in any given year.

If we can conceive of these two features of the appeals – protection and legal justice – as corresponding to different facets of justice, then the Urgent Actions appear to contain both in relatively equal measure. Although "fear for safety" percentages are always slightly higher than "bring to justice," the lines approximating the frequency of the two phrases are never far apart in either figure. Inspection of the UA document images reveals that the two kinds of phrases also differ in terms of where they appear in the texts. "Fear for safety" often appears very early in the document, when describing the specific circumstances of the person named in the Urgent Action. "Bring to justice" tends to appear later in the document, farther down on the page, when AI refers to the patterns of violations prevalent. For example, in the Urgent Action mentioned, "bring to justice" appears as part of the background information after the immediate concerns related to the individual have been detailed. Amnesty International notes that it has

> repeatedly appealed to the Salvadorian [sic] authorities to investigate and account for the thousands of detentions, "disappearances," and killings that have taken place since 1979

[26] Amnesty International. Urgent Action, "Fear of Torture/Extrajudicial Execution" (March 3, 1983, UA 50/83, AI Index no. AMR 20/05/83).

but notes in the next sentence that

> The government has . . . consistently failed to *bring those responsible to justice*. Amnesty International considers that the authorities have not once responded satisfactorily to international expressions of concern about human rights abuses.[27]

As indicated by these two different kinds of terms in its appeals, AI asks for more justice in terms of accountability at the same time that it is seeking basic protections, supporting a view of justice that maintains calls for the Samaritan-like protection characteristic of a justice of neighborhood, while also placing such care in the context of calls for the political realization of justice. It is rhetoric, certainly, but what we see in examining individual texts is that, as a group, the Urgent Actions both seek protection for an individual and also invoke the politically broader demand to bring perpetrators to justice in the national context of the country targeted by the Urgent Action.

Care and Concern versus Legal Standards in the Appeal for Justice

An intriguing opposition appears in the content of the UA appeals when considered through a justice lens. The ordinary people writing the appeals are often invited to make reference to domestic and international legal standards. Moreover, statements referring to law include not just the application of certain issues to individuals but reinforcement of existing global human rights norms, urging nation-states to recognize their obligations under international human rights law and practice. The prevalence of law is preceded in the early years, and matched in later years, by requests related to improving conditions of detention or other treatment specific to the affected person. These are

---

[27] Ibid. (emphasis added).

very direct and based on specific information about what has happened or may happen to the named individuals. On the other hand, the Urgent Actions can be very personal. Many times, the Urgent Actions also extend concern to individuals' family members and others in the affected person's circle. The Urgent Actions use phrases of concern and "fear for safety" to make this real and to recognize that the affected persons will be made safer if government officials act.

These two aspects of the Urgent Actions, standing up for both care and law, illustrate how human rights practice bridges the difference between concern for individuals within the justice of neighborhood and the political realization of justice portended by the human rights culture of argument. The Urgent Actions focus care about the unique situation of the persons named in the UA alerts, through expressions of concern about physical well-being and the identification of legal issues that need to be addressed in order for the affected persons to be protected. The one-by-one approach, which is how Urgent Actions enact the habits central to the justice of neighborhood, also increasingly invokes legal forms of justice over time. The increasing use of law alongside expressions of concern in the UA documents seems to have merged care with the political realization of justice.

Conclusion

As human rights appeals, AI's Urgent Actions are fine-grained and individually based. A broadly construed conception of justice is not evident in the appeals, which tend to use "justice" only when referring to accountability of alleged perpetrators. However, legal issues and law-related appeals permeate the document texts. Does this mean that a "thin" justice, as legal procedure, dominates the justice aspect of these documents? Although demands for procedural justice can also be indicative of the need for fuller justice, the answer is no, because indications of care and concern, part of the justice of neighborhood, are even more prevalent than procedural references. Furthermore, although citations of national law and institutions are very common, invocations of global law, specifically human rights law, rise over time. Citations of human rights norms in specific cases, as well as demands for accountability, articulate the political realization of justice in a way that reflects the potential transformation of the global sphere as a location of justice-seeking. The transnational communication and concern represented by Urgent Action as a habit of appeal support both political change and the justice of neighborhood.

Direct correspondence about human rights abuses that Urgent Actions represent is not the arena for which global human rights law was intended. However, as I have argued in this chapter, the incorporation of global law in these practical, urgent calls for justice is notable as a place to observe the contours of an emerging human rights culture of argument. I have suggested that the habitual work for justice that human rights practitioners do every day, and enable others to do, is part of the justice of neighborhood that human rights advocates have enacted globally. The Urgent Actions represent a persistent course of transnational appeal. They demonstrate not only that daily toil for justice can be transnational but that the human rights culture of argument has moved toward promotion of the political realization of justice in local contexts, while continuing to express active concern for people where they live.

6

"Together for Rights"

Oxfam and Basic Rights in Development Advocacy

To substantiate the importance of human rights, in this chapter I show how components of justice modeled in human rights practice informed innovations in global development and anti-poverty efforts, an entirely different sector of nongovernmental organization (NGO) advocacy. I illustrate the changes with a case study focused on Oxfam, a large, global anti-poverty NGO that for decades has worked to transfer aid to poor people and fight causes of poverty. In a dramatic policy overhaul in the mid-1990s, Oxfam's research and policy arm built a conceptual framework that cast anti-poverty work in light of what it called "basic rights," which referred in detail to human rights norms relevant to poverty issues and to political representation of the poor. The case study demonstrates how Oxfam transformed its approach to poverty based on the justice of neighborhood, to tap into the human rights culture of argument as a tool to spur the political realization of economic and social justice.

Like Amnesty International (AI), Oxfam has long combined the mobilization of a grassroots membership with expert research and commentary, but with a focus on problems related to poverty, hunger, and social and economic justice. Because of its size and prominence in the development field, its early rights innovations, and its history of self-conscious policy articulation, Oxfam's transition to a rights-based framework provides a strong test of the argument that human rights has become a key path to justice globally, beyond questions of civil and political repression.

126

In the 1990s and early 2000s, many NGOs in the development sector began to take a new approach to humanitarian work and emergency aid provision. In a remarkable and somewhat counterintuitive shift, Oxfam, ActionAid, and other leading development NGOs adopted human rights as a tool for their advocacy of economic and social justice. For a long time, large sections of the human rights community – both activists and scholars – had accepted that their ability to launch concrete human rights appeals on matters of economic and social equality were likely to be limited in scope. At most, they could defend individuals who were targeted for claiming such rights, but pushing for legal guarantees about the substance of economic rights was seen as problematic, for practical and conceptual reasons. Points of contention among traditional human rights NGOs like AI and Human Rights Watch included the belief that making demands about how governments should allocate their resources was especially difficult. Practical limitations included considerations of capacity, given their existing work load. Conceptually, the challenges of establishing causal responsibility for economic rights violations, as well as duties for remedy, led them to proceed with caution.[1]

At a time when the major human rights organizations were debating how and whether to integrate economic, social, and cultural (ESC) rights into their working mandates, development NGOs and affiliated actors that already worked in the field of economic and social development began to adopt human rights language. Many such groups, including Oxfam, were experienced in the delivery of humanitarian aid, having operated in the field with local NGO partners, governments, and intergovernmental organizations (IGOs) to improve and maintain economic security at the grassroots. However, Oxfam and fellow

---

[1] Curt Goering, "Amnesty International and Economic, Social, and Cultural Rights," in *Ethics in Action: The Ethical Challenges of International Human Rights Organizations*, eds. Daniel Bell and Jean-Marc Coicaud (Cambridge: Cambridge University Press, 2007), 204–217; O'Neill, "The Dark Side of Human Rights"; Roth, "Defending Economic, Social and Cultural Rights."

development-sector organizations began to devote extraordinary attention to human rights and their relation to social justice goals. The so-called rights-based approach to development incorporated civil and political rights in work for social justice by asserting the civil and political rights of people affected by poverty and injustice, and also by renewing attention to human rights principles related to economic, social, and cultural issues.

Development groups' adoption of rights-based approaches was by no means inevitable. If human rights NGOs like AI – experts in the creation and application of human rights standards – saw advocacy ESC concerns as a great challenge, why did development groups gravitate toward them so dramatically? The material and social aspects of human welfare, response to urgent material need, and provision of humanitarian aid in emergencies have always been at the crux of the work of Oxfam, ActionAid, CARE, Save the Children, and other NGOs in the development sector. All of them had turned to rights-based approaches by the early 2000s. Rights-based approaches were not an obvious choice of advocacy strategy on development issues, so what was the draw of human rights? My answer is that, despite what the classic human rights NGOs saw as the limitations of rights, the human rights culture of argument made this surprising convergence in justice-seeking practice possible.

The changes in language and practices in the development sector show how the human rights culture of argument enabled advocacy for economic and social issues beyond questions of civil and political repression. Development actors did not simply highlight economic and social rights that had previously been deemphasized by the human rights movement. They mobilized the existing human rights culture of argument to emphasize and support the political agency and civic membership of poor people in their own local neighborhoods as well as the global neighborhood. A sense of justice led them to see a need for political advocacy by and on behalf of economically disadvantaged people, and human rights provided ready resources for identifying systemic causes of poverty and standards for political remedy.

128

Background: The Rise of Rights-Based Advocacy and the International Politics of Development

In their study of rights-based advocacy, Paul Nelson and Ellen Dorsey characterize a two-part role for rights in development politics: rights provide a rationale for involving poor people in government decision-making that affects them; and they offer established global standards that lend legitimacy to policy initiatives and critiques.[2] Awareness of the tension between national economic development and attention to human well-being was not entirely new among international development actors. By the late 1980s and early 1990s at the United Nations (UN) Children's Fund (UNICEF) and the UN Development Programme, for example, practitioners concerned about poverty alleviation were using terms like "human development" and "sustainable development" to recognize the need for more than national economic development programming alone.[3] Developing countries had successfully backed a formal Declaration on the Right to Development at the UN General Assembly in 1986,[4] but implementation foundered over countries' ability and willingness to recognize actual obligations to one another. Governments in the Global North refused to meet Southern demands for concessions by industrialized states, for example.[5] When the "right to development" came up for reaffirmation in 1993 at the World Conference on Human Rights in Vienna, the importance and interdependence of all forms of individual human rights with regard to

---

[2] Nelson and Dorsey, *New Rights Advocacy*, 93.

[3] Hans-Otto Sano, "Development and Human Rights: The Necessary, but Partial Integration of Human Rights and Development," *Human Rights Quarterly* 22, no. 3 (2000): 740.

[4] "Declaration on the Right to Development" (U.N. Doc. no. A/RES/41/128, December 4, 1986).

[5] Andrea Cornwall and Celestine Nyamu-Musembi, "Putting the 'Rights-Based Approach' to Development into Perspective," *Third World Quarterly* 25, no. 8 (2004): 1422.

development were reemphasized. However, duties related to development were to be shouldered by one's own state.[6] This interpretation clarified points of potential alliance between local social movements and organizations, human rights groups, and development groups vis-à-vis governments.[7] While this was a double-edged sword that may have played down developed countries' global obligations as a matter of justice, according to one account, the focus on including states' duties toward individuals was consistent with a standard consideration of human rights' role in development. In any case, the right to development, which has been construed mainly as giving states the right to development rather than individuals, has "rarely been invoked" by social movement actors or NGOs involved in development work.[8]

Instead, NGOs engaging in international development work moved in large numbers to incorporate human rights, rather than the right to development, in their programming. Nelson and Dorsey demonstrate that ESC rights have been taken up by official development agencies in a complex variety of ways, and not only by development NGOs, as Daniel P. L. Chong has also shown.[9] Well into the twenty-first century, rights-based orientations toward development were widespread.[10] In addition, new ESC-oriented human rights organizations have sprung up

---

[6] Ibid., 1424. [7] Ibid.

[8] Peter Uvin, "From the Right to Development to the Rights-Based Approach: How 'Human Rights' Entered Development," *Development in Practice* 17, no. 4/5 (2007): 597–598.

[9] Nelson and Dorsey, *New Rights Advocacy*, 104–115. See also Daniel P. L. Chong's comparison of how subsistence rights have been approached by human rights, social justice, and humanitarian NGOs, in *Freedom from Poverty: NGOs and Human Rights Praxis* (Philadelphia: University of Pennsylvania Press, 2011).

[10] Shannon Kindornay, James Ron, and Charli Carpenter, "Rights-Based Approaches to Development: Implications for NGOs," *Human Rights Quarterly* 34, no. 2 (2012): 472–506; Paul J. Nelson and Ellen Dorsey, "Who Practices Rights-Based Development? A Progress Report on Work at the Nexus of Human Rights and Development," *World Development* 104 (2018): 97–107.

as older, traditional human rights NGOs have wrestled with how to address the full spectrum of rights.

Although a comprehensive tally of development NGOs currently influenced by a rights-based perspective would be difficult to compile, a 2018 study of a subsample of development NGOs' mission statements found that more than 28 percent (159 of 561) of international aid NGOs working in at least three countries contained human rights language.[11] As for IGOs, the UN's Sustainable Development Goals (SDGs), released in 2015, incorporated human rights concerns more fully than any previous official formulation of development recommendations for states. However, the SDGs and their predecessors, the Millennium Development Goals (MDGs), have been heavily criticized with regard to measurement and implementation when compared with human rights standards.[12]

[11] These numbers are drawn from data collected by Junhyup Kim for "To Give or to Act?" Kim coded the web-posted mission statements of international aid NGOs from seven developed countries – Australia, Canada, Japan, New Zealand, South Korea, the United Kingdom, and the USA. I am grateful to Junhyup Kim for sharing the study's original data.

[12] Although it is not possible to go into detail here, there is an extensive literature on the MDGs and their predecessors, the SDGs. For a more comprehensive list of human rights critiques of the MDGs, see Philip Alston, "Ships Passing in the Night: The Current State of the Human Rights and Development Debate Seen through the Lens of the Millennium Development Goals," *Human Rights Quarterly* 27, no. 3 (2005): 764–767. On the SDGs, see the preface to a special journal issue, Inga T. Winkler and Carmel Williams, "The Sustainable Development Goals and Human Rights: A Critical Early Review," *The International Journal of Human Rights* 21, no. 8 (2017): 1023–1028. Sakiko Fukuda-Parr has written extensively on measurement issues pertaining to human rights in the SDGs. See, for example, "International Obligations for Economic and Social Rights: The Case of the Millennium Development Goal Eight," in *Economic Rights: Conceptual, Measurement, and Policy Issues*, eds. Shareen Hertel and Lanse Minkler (New York: Cambridge University Press, 2007), 284–309.

Rights as a Path for Economic and Social Justice

When development NGOs turned to rights-based approaches, they were choosing to move from work characterized by the justice of neighborhood to pursue the political realization of justice. The human rights culture of argument that had been fostered by traditional human rights NGOs, however, developed as part of the pursuit of systematic protections for civil and political human rights, as well as acute threats to physical integrity, rather than a full realization of *social* justice. Social justice is associated with fair, shared access to a society's institutions and to institutional and material goods that are social products.[13] In common parlance, the outcomes of social justice include the ability of all to partake of the things necessary for a full life of dignity, such as adequate nutrition, access to water, a means of livelihood, a healthy environment, and access to basic health care. A long list of ESC rights is enumerated in the Universal Declaration of Human Rights and the International Covenant on Economic, Social, and Cultural Rights. It is not necessary to enumerate economic and social goods as human rights in order to recognize and campaign against patterns of deprivation or unequal access for some people but not others; however, that is what Oxfam and many other development NGOs chose to do.

Development NGOs needed to invest heavily in reframing efforts in order to adopt rights-based standards of work, despite the potential resonance of rights with the concepts related to development and humanitarian aid. For the NGO ActionAid, a rights-based approach involved a "grafting of human rights onto pre-existing ways of working" as well as work to "reimagine" organizational goals, a process that was inward-looking rather than merely instrumental.[14] Grafting can describe applying

---

[13] Johnston, *A Brief History of Justice*, 174.

[14] Paul Gready, "Organisational Theories of Change in the Era of Organisational Cosmopolitanism: Lessons from ActionAid's Human Rights-Based Approach," *Third World Quarterly* 34, no. 8 (2013): 1350.

prior norms in a way that brings a new issue into "the realm of possibility" or it can involve simply a strategic use of discourse "as a self-conscious tool."[15] Human rights gave NGOs new instruments for development advocacy, but the change entailed significant initial costs for the NGOs themselves, especially those that pioneered the approach. As will be detailed later, Oxfam spent years developing its rights-based approach.

Development NGOs were not starting from scratch: they had decades of experience and expertise in service delivery, anti-poverty advocacy, and grassroots funding, as well as involvement in IGOs. Figure 6.1 compares selected aid and development NGOs' average founding dates and dates of entry into consultative status

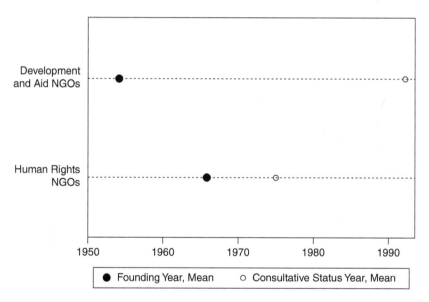

Figure 6.1 Human rights versus aid and development NGOs: Mean year of founding and consultative status

---

[15] Richard Price, "Reversing the Gun Sights: Transnational Civil Society Targets Land Mines," *International Organization* 52, no. 3 (1998): 628.

at the UN's Economic and Social Council (ECOSOC) with the average founding and consultative status dates of a selection of human rights NGOs. (Figure 6.2 lists the dates for the specific NGOs included in the sample.) Consultative status at ECOSOC, which gives NGOs access to forms of participation there, is included as a marker of engagement in global politics. The figure reveals that aid and development NGOs are generally older than their human rights counterparts, but that on average they came to ECOSOC later than their human rights colleagues. A rights-based approach would change the terms of engagement with regard to some of the prior relationships among global development NGOs and their partners in the field, and would sound an adversarial note in relationships with governments.

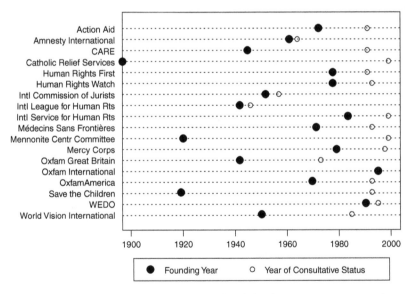

Figure 6.2 Human rights versus aid and development NGOs: Year of founding and consultative status

Aside from the necessary internal reorientation, the shift to rights required that NGOs interpret the changes for their members, especially those longtime individual supporters who still resonated with the idea of charity. ActionAid, for example, found it "easier to fundraise for child sponsorship and emergencies, people and need, than ... for human rights."[16] The same concern was cited by Ray Offenheiser, former CEO of Oxfam America, who was influential in Oxfam's global rights-based transition.[17]

A study of ActionAid cited the need, in addition, to "sell" rights-based advocacy to its partner organizations in the field.[18] A program director at Mercy Corps, a newer organization based in Portland, Oregon, mentioned that his organization's rights-aware process of involving partners in capacity planning and development entails, essentially, a form of in-kind contribution from partners, which requires a new kind of dialogue.[19] Given the required investment in such changes, it is therefore hard to imagine that the leading organizations would have taken on a rights-based approach in the absence of a deeper commitment.

NGOs focused on economic and social development already have a basic language of argument – the language of social justice – that can set economic needs, and solidarity with the poor, front and center. Solidarity rhetoric portends a fuller sense of justice, beyond the legal references and procedural justice approaches that classic human rights

---

[16] Gready, "Organisational Theories of Change in the Era of Organisational Cosmopolitanism," 1348.

[17] Raymond C. Offenheiser, interviewed by Ann Marie Clark, telephone, June 13 and 17, 2019; Chris Roche, interviewed by Ann Marie Clark, online via Zoom, June 23, 2020.

[18] Bronwen Magrath, "Global Norms, Organisational Change: Framing the Rights-Based Approach at ActionAid," *Third World Quarterly* 35, no. 7 (2014): 1273–1289.

[19] Sanjay Gurung, interviewed by Ann Marie Clark, Portland, OR, November 17, 2017. At the time of the interview, Gurung was Director of Mercy Corps Governance and Partnership Team Technical Support Unit.

actors linked to care and concern toward individuals. Why would so many of the expert aid and development organizations turn to human rights in the pursuit of social justice when expert human rights organizations saw it as a rocky path? The answer is complicated, but as the case study of Oxfam shows, it is closely related to the availability of the human rights culture of argument as a tool for the political realization of justice in the current global system.

NGOs and States: The International Context of Rights and Development Aid

Development actors did not simply highlight economic and social rights that had previously been deemphasized by the human rights movement. In claiming human rights, they made a prominent place for civil and political rights as a path toward justice for the poor. Here, I outline what the rights-based approach entails, and I trace how and why a joint emphasis on political and economic rights emerged in the case of Oxfam.

Despite considerable variation in application, what makes the rights-based approach to development distinctive is that, departing from more charity-based approaches, it uses human rights principles and strategies in the pursuit of development concerns. A rights-based approach rejects a top-down, "welfarist" conception of anti-poverty work.[20] The welfarist conception sees aid as charity, in the classic Samaritan's interpretation of neighborhood.[21] Structural understandings of poverty also cast

---

[20] Raymond C. Offenheiser and Susan H. Holcombe, "Challenges and Opportunities in Implementing a Rights-Based Approach to Development: An Oxfam America Perspective," *Nonprofit and Voluntary Sector Quarterly* 32, no. 2 (2003): 268–306.

[21] In fact, Kim finds that on average, religiously affiliated NGOs were more likely to stick with a faith-related orientation to aid as "charity," although some faith-based groups have adopted the rights-based approach. (Kim, "To Give or to Act?") World Vision is one large, international, faith-based NGO that has not adopted rights language, for example; while Catholic Relief Services has done so.

a different light on the power dynamics inherent on extending "charity" toward the poor: simple charity depends on the largesse of the "haves" toward "have-nots." Although emergency assistance can be critical in times of emergency, it is no solution to persistent structural injustice.

In the same vein, the focus of development NGOs' advocacy had sometimes made them more likely to align with, rather than challenge, the sovereignty claims of poorer states against external financial intervention, other states' power-based influence, and multinational corporations' financial heft. These considerations, in some circles, complicated the prospect of launching human rights criticisms against developing states.[22]

Rather than simply transfer aid, or assess the needs of the poor from an external perspective, the rights-based approach "promotes justice, equality and freedom and tackles the power issues that lie at the root of poverty and exploitation" using the "the standards, principles and methods of human rights, social activism and of development."[23] For the reasons cited, calls for rights also put NGOs in a more politically adversarial position. A rights-based approach builds a bridge to civil and political rights as an integral part of the development process.[24] However, it complicates some more traditional nongovernmental aid stances politically, by placing resource demands on governments and taking a stand on the accountability relations between governments and citizens.

---

[22] Offenheiser and Holcombe, "Challenges and Opportunities in Implementing a Rights-Based Approach to Development," 274.

[23] Joachim Theis, *Promoting Rights-Based Approaches: Experiences from Asia and the Pacific* (Stockholm: Save the Children, 2004), https://archive.crin.org/en/docs/reso urces/publications/hrbap/promoting.pdf, 2. Cited in Nelson and Dorsey, *New Rights Advocacy*, 93.

[24] Cornwall and Nyamu-Musembi, "Putting the 'Rights-Based Approach' to Development into Perspective," 1424.

Development advocates' turn to rights-based approaches thus marked a shift away from development as "an instrument of solidarity" between developed and developing states as well as a move away from the idea of charity underwritten by members of global civil society. Instead, new thinking about development called upon state-based duties toward citizens, and incorporated standards of development related to individuals and groups within states.[25]

By the 1990s, transnational advocacy in the human rights sphere had begun to reshape interpretations of the relationship between rights and sovereignty in international politics.[26] Standard ideas of international economic justice among nation-states implicated the global community as a whole rather than set standards for individual states. Human rights norms, in contrast, placed duties on states related to the treatment of their own inhabitants. As noted, the international solidarity demands of the right to development, and other views about the need for equitable distribution of resources among states, on the other hand, did not necessarily do so. Further, the negative repercussions of orthodox, neoliberal development models – structural adjustment and austerity measures that disproportionately affected the poor – were seen by development NGOs as part of the problem, rather than part of the solution.[27] What happened in development NGOs' turn to rights arguments is that they, like human rights NGOs, began to emphasize the rights of people and groups with regard to states' policies and development cooperation.[28] This entailed

---

[25] Sano, "Development and Human Rights," 736, 739.

[26] Kathryn Sikkink, "Human Rights, Principled Issue-Networks, and Sovereignty in Latin America," *International Organization* 47, no. 3 (1993): 411–441; Clark, *Diplomacy of Conscience.*

[27] Nelson and Dorsey, *New Rights Advocacy,* 8, 175. On the human rights effects of structural adjustment programs from 1981 through 2003, see M. Rodwan Abouharb and David Cingranelli, *Human Rights and Structural Adjustment* (Cambridge: Cambridge University Press, 2007).

[28] Although it is outside the scope of this case study, rights-based development approaches (and human rights NGOs, too) have also sought to address the human

138

recognizing and supporting the political agency of persons experiencing poverty.

NGO Relations with One Another in a Fluid Global Neighborhood

The rights-based approach became increasingly visible throughout the development sector in the late 1990s and early 2000s. The process was conditioned in part by new interactions among NGOs, staffers, and social movements working on different kinds of issues, as the story of Oxfam's transition will show. These actors learned from one another, a process intensified by the post-Cold War series of UN summits, or conferences, that took place in the 1990s on the environment, rights, women, and social issues. The conferences opened the way for encounters between global and local, large and small NGOs. Even more than for similar conferences that had been held in previous decades, these offered opportunities for NGO participation in lobbying and activities related to the official business of the conference, and at large, parallel forums created for NGOs.

The conferences contributed to a larger shift in development NGOs' dialogue over human rights. With extended exposure over the course of the conferences to the UN language endorsing ESC rights, more development NGOs "began to see rights as a lever for change."[29] New and repeated contact among NGOs also contributed to how Northern NGOs saw their own accountability and choices related to the Global North-South economic divide. The largest conferences, listed here by their nicknames, included the Earth Summit in Rio de Janeiro (1992), the World Conference on Human Rights in

rights implications of business actors. See Hertel, *Tethered Fates.* On an early effort by AI, see Nelson and Dorsey, *New Rights Advocacy,* 65–70.

[29] Offenheiser and Holcombe, "Challenges and Opportunities in Implementing a Rights-Based Approach to Development," 273.

Vienna (1993), the Social Summit in Copenhagen (1994), and the Beijing Women's Conference (1995).[30] NGOs based in Europe also found themselves meeting each other more frequently in Brussels, at meetings related to European Union (EU) concerns.

Although the UN conferences were organized by issue, some NGOs – most notably women's NGOs – advanced their agenda at multiple conferences.[31] Women organized transnationally and across issues to emphasize links between human rights, gender, the environment, and development. Activists in the global women's movement had worked in the 1970s and 1980s to bridge North-South divides within the movement and to arrive at a jointly held, gendered critique of development practice.[32] The UN Convention on the Elimination of Discrimination against Women in 1981 had set standards for the treatment of women that foretold later links between human rights and development, by emphasizing state responsibility for women's legal protection.[33] Global women's advocates also learned from the human rights movement in the 1970s and 1980s and, by the 1990s, had chosen to adopt human rights language more explicitly with regard to violence and economic issues affecting women.[34] The slogan advanced at the

[30] The official names and dates of these conferences were, respectively, UN Conference on Environment and Development, Rio de Janeiro, June 3–14, 1992; the World Conference on Human Rights, Vienna, June 14–25, 1993; the International Conference on Population and Development, Cairo, September 5–13, 1994; the World Summit for Social Development, Copenhagen, March 6–12, 1995; and the Fourth World Conference on Women, Beijing, September 4–15, 1995. Four other conferences were held in that decade: on education (Jomtien, 1990); children (New York, 1990); human settlements (Istanbul, 1996); and food (Rome, 1996).

[31] Friedman, Hochstetler, and Clark, *Sovereignty, Democracy, and Global Civil Society.*

[32] For details, see Friedman, "Gendering the Agenda," 317–318.

[33] "Convention on the Elimination of All Forms of Discrimination against Women" (1249 U.N.T.S. 13; 19 I.L.M. 33 [1980], entered into force September 3, 1981).

[34] Ellen Dorsey, "The Global Women's Movement: Articulating a New Vision of Global Governance," in *The Politics of Global Governance: International Organizations in an Interdependent World,* ed. Paul F. Diehl (Boulder, CCO: Lynne

UN's 1993 World Conference on Human Rights that "women's rights are human rights," implied that ESC rights, including gender-based considerations related to development issues, needed further integration into broader human rights claims and development programming.

Oxfam and Basic Rights against Poverty: "Words into Action"

Oxfam was the first NGO to engage with the broad spectrum of human rights in pursuit of social justice, making it a critical case for understanding how and why human rights principles came to inform the pursuit of justice in development work. Oxfam had logged considerable experience, research, and reflection on the causes of poverty. At the same time, Oxfam was influenced by encounters with thinkers and practitioners outside of the organization. After providing basic background on Oxfam's organizational context, I detail its transition to a language of rights.

Oxfam Great Britain and the Other Oxfams

The original Oxfam in Great Britain, now called Oxfam GB, remains by far the largest Oxfam, and it predates Oxfam International, although to talk about Oxfam now is to refer to a collective: nineteen national Oxfam organizations, and Oxfam International. In 1995, eight national Oxfam organizations created Oxfam International as a confederation, united by a common strategic plan. Before then, national Oxfams operated independently, with no central governing structure.[35] Oxfam International's offices remained in Oxford until 2018, when the

---

Rienner Publishers, 2001), 441–444; Htun and Weldon, *The Logics of Gender Justice*, 51–83.

[35] On the decision to confederate, see Wong, *Internal Affairs*, 121–122.

headquarters moved to Nairobi.[36] Oxfam International's 2018–2019 Annual Report listed 245 international headquarters staff, with 52 based at the International Secretariat in Nairobi, 59 still in Oxford, and others at Oxfam International offices elsewhere,[37] but in the wake of the COVID pandemic, Oxfam announced a reorganization with sizeable cutbacks to personnel and programs globally.[38]

To understand how human rights became part of Oxfam's working agenda, it is necessary to start with Oxfam GB, which is still the largest and most powerful of the Oxfams. Oxfam GB was instrumental in mounting Oxfam's "Together for Rights" campaign in the mid-1990s. Oxfam International formally adopted a rights-based framework in 2001, but the conceptual and practical groundwork was laid during the 1990s.

As shown in Table 6.1, Oxfam GB has remained much larger than any other Oxfam affiliate. In 1991, it employed about 1,700 people, with 12 local offices in the UK and Ireland, and 34 field offices overseas.[39] Its national network of Oxfam shops, selling donated goods, books, and retail fair trade items, and staffed mainly by volunteers, continues to lend it a great deal of public loyalty and legitimacy within the United

---

[36] Oxfam International, *Oxfam Annual Report, April 2017–March 2018* (Oxford: Oxfam International, 2019), 8.

[37] Oxfam International, *Fighting Inequality to Beat Poverty, Annual Report, 2018–19* (Oxford: Oxfam International, 2019), 47.

[38] At the time of writing, Oxfam International's cuts were expected to affect 1,450 people out of approximately 5,000 Oxfam program staff globally. See Peter Beaumont, "Oxfam to Close in 18 Countries and Cut 1,500 Staff Amid Coronavirus Pressures," *The Guardian*, May 20, 2020. Oxfam GB was also expecting cuts; see Karen McVeigh, "Oxfam Funding Crisis Puts 200 UK Jobs at Risk," *The Guardian*, June 4, 2020. In the year or two before the pandemic, the organization had weathered criticism, regulatory penalties, and a review of its procedures after it was reported in 2018 that Oxfam GB's operation had not properly supervised and disciplined aid workers who had paid for sex with minors in Haiti after the 2010 earthquake there.

[39] Maggie Black, *Oxfam: The First Fifty Years* (Oxford: Oxfam, 1992), 293.

Table 6.1 *Comparative staff sizes: Oxfam GB, Oxfam America, and Oxfam Novib*

Oxfam affiliate	1990s employees	Early 2020 employees
Oxfam GB (Oxford)	1,700 in 1991[41]	2,040 in 2020[42]
Oxfam America (Boston)	83 in 1998[43]	326 in 2018[44]
Oxfam Novib (The Hague)	251 in 1996[45]	325 in 2020[46]

Note: Totals exclude overseas-based staff.

Kingdom. In comparison, Oxfam America, based in Boston, was in 1998 a tiny operation of fewer than 90 employees in its Boston and Washington, DC offices and 27 employees across its 7 overseas field offices. Oxfam Novib, based in The Hague, had a staff of 251 in 1996, and is the most powerful and influential Oxfam in Europe outside of the United Kingdom.[40]

In light of Oxfam GB's strength as a star in the constellation of other British NGOs, it seems a somewhat unlikely case for a turn to rights. First, it was practically next door to AI, which had been

[40] For sources of data in this paragraph on staff sizes, see notes to Table 6.1.

[41] Black, *Oxfam*. [42] See McVeigh, "Oxfam Funding Crisis Puts 200 UK Jobs at Risk."

[43] Oxfam America, *Annual Report* (Boston: Oxfam America, 1998), 39.

[44] Oxfam America, "Audited Financial Statements and Form 990: Federal Form 990-2018," https://webassets.oxfamamerica.org/media/documents/OXFAM_AMERIC A_INC_-_2018_990.pdf?_gl=1*1x3uwh7*_ga*MTIoNTg2Mjc4NC4xNjI2ODAyNz M3*_ga_R58YETD6XK*MTYyNjgwMjczNy4xLjAuMTYyNjgwMjc2Ny4w.

[45] J. J. M. Onderwater, *Working for Development: An Enquiry into the Potential Need for University Training Programmes in Development Projects* (Groningen, Germany: Pro Human Project, Office for International Cooperation, University of Groningen, 1997); as cited in Hans-Paul Klinjsma and Caspar Schweigman, "Country Report: Netherlands," in *Humanitarian Development Studies in Europe*, eds. Julia González, Wilhelm Löwenstein, and Mo Malek (Bilbao: University of Deusto, 1999), 199.

[46] Oxfam Novib, *Annual Report 2018–19* (The Hague: Oxfam Novib, 2020), 53.

recognized as a key global human rights organization for years before Oxfam began to contemplate a rights approach. Oxfam's main public collaboration with AI had involved a ten-year joint campaign, eventually bringing in other NGOs, for a treaty limiting the trade in small arms. Oxfam's rationale for involvement in that campaign did not stem directly from the human rights implications but from Oxfam's recognition of poverty's enduring relation to armed conflict.[47] Oxfam did share a social milieu with AI that was characteristically British, according to Sarah Stroup, but also characteristic of the Quaker, and other, faith traditions held by some of Oxfam and AI's founders. Stroup characterizes these faith traditions as commonly testifying that individuals can "work voluntarily to change the society around them."[48] But despite common British origins, the two organizations have maintained very distinct programs as well as separate, if sometimes overlapping, constituencies.[49]

Second, within the options available to British NGOs working in the development sector, an unqualified rights approach could have had significant fiscal repercussions for Oxfam GB. In UK charity law,

---

[47] Duncan Green and Anna Macdonald, "Power and Change: The Arms Trade Treaty" (Oxford: Oxfam GB for Oxfam International, 2015), https://oxfamilibrary .openrepository.com/bitstream/handle/10546/338471/cs-arms-trade-treaty-160115- en.pdf?sequence=1&isAllowed=y.

[48] Sarah S. Stroup, *Borders among Activists: International NGOs in the United States, Britain, and France* (Ithaca, NY: Cornell University Press, 2012), 191. On Oxfam and Quakers, see also Black, *Oxfam*, 81. On AI and the religious affiliations of its founders, see Stephen Hopgood, *Keepers of the Flame: Understanding Amnesty International* (Ithaca, NY: Cornell University Press, 2006), 57–58.

[49] In an exception at the local level, for a number of years, Amnesty International Belgium and Oxfam Belgium have sponsored a joint annual day of action for high-school–based Oxfam and AI groups, "OxfAMnesty," and some of the groups themselves are jointly organized as OxfAMnesty groups. See, for example, Amnesty International, "Education: OxfAMnesty Activists Join Forces for Women's Rights – Belgium" (2013), www.amnesty.org/en/latest/education/2013/09/oxfamnesty-activists-join-forces-for-womens-rights-belgium/.

human rights promotion is considered a form of political advocacy, which is not protected by charity law.[50] By adopting a rights approach, Oxfam GB risked losing its charity status, which comes with considerable tax concessions. The move to rights required a "massive organizational change" that included not only changes to the organization's constitution but also to the way that it related to government regulations and to its beneficiaries, according to Oxfam's legal officer.[51] To this day, Oxfam GB's strategies pertaining to advocacy for rights must be carefully and deliberately articulated with regard to Oxfam's aid and development objectives lest they be judged as incorporating political activities not related to the organization's central charitable purpose.[52]

Even before linking human rights to its development work, Oxfam GB walked a delicate line between funding programs for poverty alleviation and what was seen as political advocacy. The potential risks came to a head when Oxfam GB was censured in 1991 by the official Charity Commission for England and Wales, for activities related to its 1988 campaign on Cambodia that were judged to be too political.[53] This feature of British charity law made it all the more unlikely that a group with Oxfam's focus on poverty would choose to link its work to a human rights framework without a strong rationale.

The need for social justice as a solution to poverty was that rationale. Because of its history, Oxfam's origins and identity were strongly tied to provision of aid and emergency relief. Already by the 1980s, global poverty relief and a turn toward critique of the impact on poor people of global aid, trade, and debt were central to Oxfam's

---

[50] Mike Parkinson, interviewed by Ann Marie Clark, Oxford, January 24, 2018. See also Deborah Eade, Suzanne Williams, and Oxfam, *The Oxfam Handbook of Development and Relief*, three vols. (Oxford: Oxfam, 1995), 27.

[51] Parkinson, January 24, 2018.

[52] In comparison, because of AI's human rights work, not all of AI's activities qualify as charitable.

[53] Black, *Oxfam*, 283.

work.[54] But, as the 1995 *Oxfam Poverty Report* argued, emergency solutions and need-based aid could not address the causes of poverty.[55]

Oxfam, Poverty, and Rights

The poverty report was issued in the midst of Oxfam GB's move to public identification of anti-poverty work with rights. Authored by Kevin Watkins, then-Head of Oxfam Research, the report mentions the Universal Declaration of Human Rights on the first page, proclaiming that "never again should governments relinquish responsibility for protecting the most basic social and economic rights of their citizens," and observes in a section on "the need for a renewed vision" that "much of the overall framework for translating social and economic rights from principle into practice already exists" in the UN Charter, the Universal Declaration of Human Rights, and the International Covenant on Economic, Social and Cultural Rights.[56]

Oxfam GB's large and influential research and policy arm produced the conceptual work on poverty and rights that became foundational for Oxfam International. As the brain behind Oxfam's initial conceptualization of how rights could inform its anti-poverty work, Oxfam GB crafted a critical stance on development that was philosophically linked to principles of justice; namely that global economic and social structures were unjustly stacked against the poor and complicit in the perpetuation of poverty. Justice demanded equity, not only the distributional equity that meshes well with

---

[54] Ibid.

[55] Kevin Watkins and Oxfam GB, *The Oxfam Poverty Report* (Oxford: Oxfam GB, 1995). A later report on education, also by Watkins, rooted education issues in both ESC rights and political rights. *The Oxfam Education Report* (Oxford: Oxfam GB, 2000).

[56] Watkins and Oxfam GB, *The Oxfam Poverty Report*, 1, 7.

economic and social human rights but equal political participation and gender equity, which fall more traditionally within the purview of civil and political rights.

Although human rights advocacy in support of global development concerns became a system-wide feature of NGO and IGO approaches after the turn of the century, Oxfam's transition to incorporation of rights was the most comprehensive and transparent.[57] Large NGOs that mirrored Oxfam's shift at about the same time, or shortly thereafter, included Save the Children, CARE, and ActionAid.[58]

How Oxfam Moved to New Applications of Human Rights for Social Justice

Well into the twenty-first century, it is almost forgotten that the 1990s was a time of new optimism about global cooperation. With the fall of the Berlin Wall in 1989 and the end of the Cold War, people in the development world perceived an opportunity to reground the premises even of official development aid to something more related to justice and less related to geopolitics. At Oxfam, there was a sense of hope "spilling back in through people in the field" that economic and development aid's role as a political instrument of the Cold War could be shifted in favor of efforts to eradicate poverty.[59] Although Oxfam International was not yet a reality when Oxfam GB began to work on rights issues, discussion was increasing among the Oxfams and other

[57] Nelson and Dorsey, *New Rights Advocacy*. See ibid., table 3.1 comparing Oxfam with CARE, Save the Children, and ActionAid, 115.

[58] For a discussion of ActionAid, which formally adopted a rights-based approach in 1998, see Matilda Aberese Ako, Nana Akua Anyidoho, and Gordon Crawford, "NGOs, Rights-Based Approaches and the Potential for Progressive Development in Local Contexts: Constraints and Challenges in Northern Ghana," *Journal of Human Rights Practice* 5, no. 1 (2013): 46–74.

[59] Feeney, June 1, 2020.

European aid agencies about how they might collaborate at the EU in Brussels, and at the UN. A similar sense of potential for new attention to human rights, as well as economic and social issues, infused the UN agenda.

Guided in its approach to the UN meetings by Patricia Feeney, who moved from AI to Oxfam GB as Senior Policy Advisor in 1990, Oxfam lobbied for the importance of rights to just development at the UN global conferences. Feeney had served as a Latin America researcher at AI since 1975. By 1990, many countries in the region were transitioning to democratic rule. South American countries were seeing a lower incidence of large-scale state-sponsored violence and direct repression. However, the costs of governments' economic development policies in the region were falling disproportionately on less well-off countries and on certain groups within those countries: on the poor, on women, and on indigenous groups. These justice-related concerns generally fell outside of AI's purview, but squarely within Oxfam's. Feeney became interested in "how the anti-poverty agenda could be infused with a human rights perspective" as Oxfam developed a new approach to advocacy.[60]

Feeney recalled that she arrived at Oxfam at a time when the organization employed "many gifted writers" and thinkers able to articulate new principles for Oxfam's historic anti-poverty work. Oxfam's legacy of attention to "power, . . . injustice," and an awareness that accountability of governments and non-state actors on development required "participation, discussion on equity, [and] mobilization" was compatible with "a non-legalistic understanding of human rights," reflected Chris Roche, who joined Oxfam's policy team in 1994.[61] Still others within Oxfam looked to humanitarian law for protecting rights in conflict zones.[62] Feeney had brought an

---

[60] Ibid. [61] Roche, June 23, 2020. [62] Offenheiser, June 13 and 17, 2019.

additional commitment to a legal understanding of human rights, according to Roche.[63]

In the years after Feeney arrived, the Oxfam policy team began considering more deliberately how to situate its work in a rights framework. Despite her leadership in helping to bring relevant rights concerns to Oxfam's work, including advocacy at the UN summits, Feeney claimed to have been "a very small cog in the Oxfam machine."[64] Whether or not she underestimates her contribution, Feeney's story, and Oxfam's more broadly, illustrates a changing awareness that rights could be a tool for helping to meet the demands of a broader sense of social justice.

Feeney had witnessed the widespread use of torture and disappearances while working as AI's Argentina researcher during the country's "dirty war" initiated by the right-wing military coup in 1976. The challenges for justice in Latin America were shifting by the late 1980s, with a wave of democratization in the Americas. The 1980s also had seen the widespread application of neoliberal austerity measures recommended by international financial institutions to deal with the Latin American debt crisis. Such measures included policies that mandated cuts in government subsidies to food and other necessities, for example, which had a heavy impact on the poor. This was happening in tandem with permissive government policies favoring development projects and private expansion of landholdings. Feeney's research portfolio at AI turned toward the Amazon region.

> I was doing a lot of work with colleagues at Amnesty on the rural violence in Brazil and across the Amazon – displacement of poor peasant farmers and encroachments on indigenous people's lands.[65]

In the Brazilian state of Roraima, for example, gold mining was displacing the Yanomami people, much of it "either overtly or covertly

[63] Roche, June 23, 2020. [64] Feeney, June 1, 2020. [65] Ibid.

promoted by the local authorities, landowners, and at times the federal authorities."[66] Development-induced displacement was

> a fairly straightforward example of a human rights issue ... where there might be an overriding reason to move people, but that doesn't remove their rights to have proper compensation or protections, [and] to be properly informed [of] what was even happening. Often, the first they knew was when a bulldozer appeared on horizon.[67]

After the work on torture and disappearances, immediate physical security issues that had characterized the work on Latin America in her initial years at AI, Feeney became interested in the human rights effects of poverty and development as more long-term, persistent problems. As with the displacement example, economic development models and trade policies could have acute impacts on human rights.

Despite AI's official recognition that all human rights were "indivisible," its mandate restricted its active work to civil and political rights, especially in the pre-1990 period.[68] Within AI staff and membership, questions about whether to relax AI's mandate and how best to use its resources were ongoing, and had always been there to some degree.[69] A sense of justice almost predictably would beg the question of whether and how to extend the human rights culture of argument to broader justice issues. In addition, environmental activism by other NGOs was beginning to link environmental concerns, development, and indigenous land rights as pressing issues in the late 1980s.

Oxfam in 1990 thus offered a wider berth from which to study and act on problems of poverty and economic development, which Feeney perceived in human rights terms as well as economic terms.

---

[66] Ibid. [67] Ibid.

[68] Peter R. Baehr, "Amnesty International and Its Self-imposed Limited Mandate," *Netherlands Quarterly of Human Rights* 12, no. 1 (1994): 5–21.

[69] See also Buchanan, *Amnesty International and Human Rights Activism in Postwar Britain.*

Despite the uncertainty within human rights circles about how to address economic inequities with rights language, someone like Feeney had, in a sense, lived the construction of the human rights culture of argument as a tool for justice, extending as it did from principles of concern to justiciability through law.

The Latin American experience with rights and politics was by no means unique to Patricia Feeney. Perhaps because of Latin America's experience with authoritarianism, within Oxfam, staff who had field experience in Latin America tended to be especially adamant, even "radical," about the importance of bringing a new view to the links between poverty and development, former staffer Chris Roche recalled.[70] Human rights activists of the early 1990s had cut their teeth on Latin American developments. As Feeney's example shows, as those activists and development workers gained experience, they were poised to provide leadership.

Although the basics of human rights practice had been established by the 1990s, rights had not been fully articulated – by rights groups themselves – with regard to a broader sense of justice. Feeney was well equipped to see the ways rights applied to broader justice issues. She had deep contacts with the other professionals in the human rights movement, and the time was ripe for cross-fertilization.

Feeney attended both the 1992 Earth Summit at Rio, and the 1993 World Conference on Human Rights as part of Oxfam's delegations. Oxfam GB coordinated its approach to the Earth Summit at Rio with several other national Oxfams.[71] It was not unusual for NGOs from one sector to attend more than just one of the themed conferences. However, the rights conference did not see many development NGOs in attendance, according to Feeney. Oxfam's small delegation to Vienna organized a session on development-induced displacement.

[70] Roche, June 23, 2020. [71] Wong, *Internal Affairs*, 121.

The Vienna conference helped to build a basis for rights as a path to justice in another way, by forcing the issue of North-South differences on development and rights. In the face of initiatives by a number of governments of developing countries to question the universality of human rights, and with renewed states' attention to a right to development, NGOs at Vienna, including the mainstream ones, presented a united front of commitment to the universal and "integrated" nature of all form of rights.[72] There were still some North-South differences among NGOs. According to one account, the large human rights NGOs' seeming aloofness toward promotion of ESC rights "began to change" at Vienna.[73] The conference not only highlighted similarities and differences in NGOs' issue positions but they specifically problematized North-South differences on human rights, which also relate to how development is conceptualized. As a group, the UN conferences engendered some conflict but also the development of alliances and common strategies. Nelson and Dorsey emphasize that the conferences "deepened northern NGOs' exposure to southern NGOs, some of which had worked more seamlessly at the nexus of human rights and development for a decade or more."[74]

From the vantage point of development NGOs, the March 1995 Social Summit in Copenhagen was the key conference of the 1990s. It was at this conference that a coalition of NGOs concerned with economic and social development lobbied for greater attention to ESC rights. Feeney crafted Oxfam's strategy for the Social Summit, which included working with a set of European development NGOs (now ACORD) on a joint lobbying position related to human rights.[75] The Netherlands' Oxfam organization, Oxfam Novib, was well funded and

---

[72] Clark, Friedman, and Hochstetler, "The Sovereign Limits of Global Civil Society."

[73] Ako, Anyidoho, and Crawford, "NGOs, Rights-Based Approaches and the Potential for Progressive Development in Local Contexts," 47. See also Clark, Friedman, and Hochstetler, "The Sovereign Limits of Global Civil Society."

[74] Nelson and Dorsey, *New Rights Advocacy*, 31. [75] Feeney, June 1, 2020.

eager to collaborate with Oxfam GB on common issues at the UN summits.[76] In 1994, at the second official UN preparatory meeting for the Social Summit, held in New York, Feeney represented Oxfam in UN-level lobbying with other NGOs to urge that the conference declaration include recommendations for taking social needs into account in International Monetary Fund and World Bank programs, including structural adjustment policies, as well as scrutiny of the new World Trade Organization, and stronger recognition of the legally binding nature of the International Covenant on Economic, Social and Cultural Rights.[77] At the summit itself, a caucus of development NGOs, humanitarian relief NGOs, and smaller movement-based NGOs from the Global South campaigned together on the importance of human rights to development processes.[78] Oxfam's contemporaneous campaigning newsletter reported to its members that the Social Summit "had aimed 'to do for poverty what Rio did for the environment' and put economic and social rights on the world agenda." The article, entitled, "Fine Words, Shame About the Action," lamented the fact that more concrete commitments by governments did not emerge.[79]

Oxfam's mobilization around rights continued at the Beijing Women's Conference in September 1995. Oxfam called for action to recognize and foster women's basic rights to equality, specifically improved access to education and health services for women in the context of structural adjustment policies, and declared that

---

[76] Ibid.

[77] Oxfam GB, "Social Development Summit," in *The Big Idea: The Newsletter for Oxfam's New Campaign, Issue no. 4* (Oxford: Oxford University, Bodleian Library [September 29, 1994]).

[78] See Cornwall and Nyamu-Musembi, "Putting the 'Rights-Based Approach' to Development into Perspective," 1423; Ako, Anyidoho, and Crawford, "NGOs, Rights-Based Approaches and the Potential for Progressive Development in Local Contexts," 47–48.

[79] Oxfam GB, "Copenhagen Summit: Fine Words, Shame About the Action," in *Oxfam Campaigner* no. 15 (Summer 1995): 1.

governments should direct more social services toward women. They also added their support for international recognition of women's rights as human rights.[80]

Building a Rights-Based Approach within Oxfam

As already seen, Oxfam used the UN conferences to lobby for increased recognition of the importance of economic, social, and cultural human rights norms at the global level. Such rights were consonant with Oxfam's knowledge about the intersection of rights with development needs, and Oxfam urged governments to recognize existing norms related to ESC rights. As justice work, the conference-based advocacy represents a turn toward the human rights culture of argument to appeal for attention to development concerns using existing norms. Meanwhile, Oxfam began designing a way to link its working approach to human rights.

In 1994 Oxfam UK and Ireland, now known as Oxfam GB,[81] organized a campaign at home that would feature rights as part of a thoroughgoing reconceptualization of its anti-poverty approach, rooted in a conception of "Basic Rights." Oxfam GB's "Together for Rights" campaign launched in 1995. "Together for Rights" was the first public articulation of appeals to human rights by a major, globally focused NGO engaged in development work. Oxfam GB's policy department did the conceptual "homework" on the move to this approach, coordinating an intensive effort in the late 1990s to develop principles to drive Oxfam International's work under a rights-based approach.

---

[80] Oxfam GB, "'Together for Rights, Together against Poverty,' an Agenda for Equality: Oxfam at the Beijing Women's Conference," *Oxfam Campaigner* no. 16 (Autumn 1995): 2.

[81] I refer to the British Oxfam by its current name, Oxfam GB.

Oxfam created what it called a "Global Charter for Basic Rights" to ground its advocacy globally and nationally. Without these rights, Oxfam said, "people will never be able to work their way out of poverty." Oxfam has been described as having taken an idiosyncratic approach to rights, but the covering language of basic rights was clearly rooted in international human rights. In preparatory materials for Oxfam activists, the charter was described as a "reaffirmation of the basic rights of every human being as enshrined in the Universal Declaration of Human Rights, 50 years ago."[82]

Oxfam's "Basic Rights" campaign promoted basic rights derived from global human rights standards, but did not involve an explicit legal strategy. This marks a contrast with how AI had developed its global anti-torture campaign. Almost twenty years earlier, AI had documented torture and connected it to public appeals, while also developing and promoting international legal standards on torture that could then be invoked in both public appeals and expert inter-governmental bodies. Oxfam's campaign built a platform of basic rights that people are "born with" and "the world's governments have signed up to."[83] It just so happened that the bulk of these were economic and social rights enshrined in the Universal Declaration of Human Rights and in the International Covenant on Economic, Social, and Cultural Rights.

Human rights provided the new argument for Oxfam's work to address the causes of poverty. Aid or sharing with those in need was not just an option for the well-off. Instead, poverty was a systematic violation of poor people's basic rights that should be addressed by strengthening respect for those rights. Materials from

---

[82] Oxfam GB, "'Together for Rights, Together against Poverty,' Southern Launches: Demands of the Poor Should Be Heard," *Oxfam Campaigner* no. 16 (Autumn 1995): 2.

[83] Pat Simmons, *Words into Action: Basic Rights and the Campaign against World Poverty* (Oxford: Oxfam UK and Ireland, 1995).

Oxfam GB's archives, and interviews with several former staffers, show that Oxfam made detailed plans to reground its work by building an argument for just, human-centered economic development based on human rights standards. To do so, Oxfam looked not only to law but also to certain philosophers whose work linked rights conceptions with issues that resonated with development. This would not have been unusual among the well-educated staffers of Oxfam GB's policy shop.

Oxfam's formulation centered on what it called "basic rights." The idea of basic rights included selected civil and political rights, but also built on a sense that rights protections should include the full spectrum of rights claims. The philosopher Henry Shue had argued that people's basic rights are of two kinds: subsistence rights and security rights, both necessary for access to all other rights.[84] *Words into Action*, the Oxfam report issued at the start of the campaign, noted that

> [t]he rights highlighted in the Charter ... represent those which Oxfam believes to be the most basic rights of all – to subsistence and security – without which other rights are unattainable.[85]

This definition mirrors the definition in Shue's book on basic rights: "rights are basic ... if enjoyment of them is essential to the enjoyment of all other rights."[86] For Shue, the right to physical security is uncontroversial and involves the basic right "not to be subjected to murder, torture, mayhem, rape, or assault."[87] Subsistence rights, for Shue, involve "minimal economic security," including "unpolluted air, unpolluted water, adequate food, adequate clothing, adequate shelter, and minimal preventive public health care," or "a decent chance at a reasonably healthy and active life of more or less normal length."[88]

---

[84] Henry Shue, *Basic Rights: Subsistence, Affluence, and U.S. Foreign Policy* (Princeton, NJ: Princeton University Press, 1980).

[85] Simmons, *Words into Action*, 6. [86] Shue, *Basic Rights*, 19. [87] Ibid., 20.

[88] Ibid., 23.

The basic rights that Oxfam laid out were somewhat more extensive. Shue had not explicitly included freedom of assembly and some other political and civil rights in the list of basic rights. Instead, he cast the basic right to physical security as a constitutive part of other political rights, such as freedom of assembly, which could not be exercised fully without the right to physical security.[89]

Although I was unable to find explicit references to Shue in the Oxfam archives, Feeney confirmed that "some of us were reading Shue."[90] The economist and philosopher Amartya Sen's writing on development also influenced members of Oxfam's policy circle in formulating the transition to a rights-based approach. Several clippings from Sen's public writings in this period appear in the correspondence files of policy team member Chris Roche at the Oxfam GB archives. In an essay responding to the heated debate at the 1993 World Conference on Human Rights, in which a group of developing states sought to pit development imperatives against civil and political rights guarantees, Sen asserted the vital importance of civil and political rights in maintaining an accountability relationship between governments and people. For this reason, he argued, the civil and political rights guarantees inherent in democracy promote successful economic and social development. Not only that, but rights were constitutive of development, he argued: having a voice in deliberations was essential even to conceptualizing economic needs.[91]

Oxfam policy makers resonated with these views of rights as basic components of social justice more broadly. Roche recalled Sen's stopping by the offices of Oxfam GB "when he was in Oxford to give a talk."[92] As an indication that Oxfam at this time was engaged with

[89] Ibid., 26–27. [90] Feeney, June 1, 2020.
[91] Amartya Sen, "Freedoms and Needs," *New Republic*, January 1994: 31–38; and more extensively, see Amartya Sen, *Development as Freedom* (Oxford: Oxford University Press, 1999).
[92] Roche, June 23, 2020.

ideas related to aspects of rights, justice, and law, Feeney noted that both Sen and Philip Alston, the distinguished human rights lawyer and scholar whose expertise includes poverty, spoke at an early training session on human rights for Oxfam staff.[93]

In a sign of the importance of his views, Sen was named "honorary president" of Oxfam International from 2000 to 2002.[94] The appointment coincided with Oxfam International's official incorporation of rights in its 2001–2004 strategic plan, which nods to Sen as having argued that "the achievement of civil and political rights also has an instrumental relationship with poverty eradication and equitable economic development."[95]

As indicated by the invitation extended to Philip Alston, Oxfam was also paying attention to the relation of legal human rights standards to poverty. During the period of his visit to Oxfam, Alston would have been a member of the UN Committee on Economic, Social, and Cultural Rights, which is the body responsible for monitoring the International Covenant on Economic, Social, and Cultural Rights.[96] More recently, Alston held the mandate of UN Special Rapporteur on Extreme Poverty and Human Rights, from 2014 to 2020, bringing human rights to bear on extreme poverty not only in poorer states but in wealthy states like the USA and Britain.[97]

---

[93] Feeney, June 1, 2020.

[94] Amartya Sen, "Curriculum Vitae: Amartya Sen," Harvard University, https://scholar.harvard.edu/files/sen/files/cv_sen_amartya_jan2013_0.pdf.

[95] Oxfam International, *Towards Global Equity: Strategic Plan, 2001–2004* (Oxford: Oxfam International, 2001). The plan cites Sen's 1999 *Development as Freedom* in section 2, aim 4.

[96] New York University, "Biography: Philip G. Alston, New York University Faculty of Law," https://its.law.nyu.edu/facultyprofiles/index.cfm?fuseaction=profile.biography&personid=19742.

[97] See, for example, Ceylan Yeginsu, "U.K. Austerity Has Inflicted 'Great Misery,' U.N. Official Says," *New York Times*, May 22, 2019; UN Office of the High Commissioner

The Campaign for Basic Rights: *Words into Action*

The focus of the campaign for basic rights, launched by Oxfam GB in 1995, was the application of a rights perspective to issues central to human well-being. Oxfam consciously connected a rights perspective to political change as well as economic change. The title of the campaign was "Together for Rights, Together against Poverty." Oxfam demurred from engaging the questions that would soon dog the classic human rights organizations about whether their human rights methodology could be effective in economic, social, and cultural human rights standards. Instead, Oxfam centered its focus on how rights applied to issues of poverty.

Oxfam's public materials relied explicitly on human rights norms and empirical information. The Global Charter for Basic Rights introduced in Oxfam's *Words into Action* lists ten basic rights: the right to (1) a home; (2) clean water; (3) enough to eat; (4) a safe environment; (5) protection from violence; (6) equality of opportunity; (7) a say in one's future (i.e., voting, political participation, freedom of assembly, and freedom of expression); (8) an education; (9) a livelihood; (10) health care.[98] *Words into Action* includes a two-page list of international agreements on human rights that contains the standard treaties, but begins with the UN charter's declaration that human rights are the responsibility of all UN members, and ends with a synopsis of the UN Social Summit in Copenhagen's Declaration on Social Development, which

> affirms the agreement of governments to take action aimed at promoting social justice, solidarity, and equality; defines poverty not simply as a lack of income resulting in hunger, ill health,

for Human Rights, "Statement on Visit to the USA, by Professor Philip Alston, United Nations Special Rapporteur on Extreme Poverty and Human Rights" (December 15, 2017), www.ohchr.org/EN/NewsEvents/Pages/DisplayNews.aspx? NewsID=22533&LangID=E.

[98] Pat Simmons, "The Oxfam Global Charter for Basic Rights," in *Words into Action*, 5.

homelessness, and limited access to education, but as being inextricably linked to a lack of control over resources, including land, skills, knowledge, capita, and social connections; [and] states that the eradication of poverty "will require democratic participation and changes in economic structures to ensure access for all to resources."[99]

"Recognized – Denied – But Possible"

Words into Action systematically presents each of the ten rights in three sections: "Recognized – Denied – But Possible." As an introduction to each right, the report lists where and how the right has been "recognized" by governments in international law. For the "Recognized" section on the right to enough to eat, for example, Oxfam lists three international legal norms: the International Covenant on Economic, Social, and Cultural Rights' guarantee of an adequate standard of living and the right to be free from hunger; the text of the then-recently opened Convention on the Rights of the Child pledging action against child malnutrition; and the Geneva Conventions' prohibition of starvation as an instrument of war. A second section, "Denied," offers a bulleted list of ways in which the named right is not respected, along with an illustrated inset describing one situation in more detail. For the right to enough to eat, the report features Bweri, a village in Tanzania, whose residents cannot feed themselves. Bweri is home to a fish-packing business but, the inset notes, the company's exports had reduced the villagers' own access to protein. Among other featured statistics is the figure that, globally, 800 million people were "severely malnourished or starving." A third section, "But Possible," features an illustration of positive change at the local level when people are able to act in a way that exercises the right. In this section, the illustrations again focus on developing countries.

[99] Ibid., 36–37.

A Kenyan small farmer trained to raise sorghum with her family through a cooperative community venture, as part of the "Lokitaung Pastoral Development Project," is featured under the right to enough to eat.[100] The report emphasizes that poverty tends to be a result of the denial of many basic rights, not just one: "we have to plan for a world where the *whole body* of basic rights is recognized and put into place."[101] The rights are invoked as a call to the actions needed by governments to provide for "opportunity," "participation," "a fair distribution of wealth and power," "peace and security," and "a safe environment."[102] In a section urging members to take part in campaigning where they live, examples of "thinking globally, acting locally" in the cities of Oxford and Manchester appear.[103] The last item in the report is the full text of the Universal Declaration of Human Rights.

Although the large human rights NGOs may have been wary of expanding their rights mandates in the 1990s, Oxfam, and other development NGOs saw rights language as an opportunity to add meaning and calls for accountability. For Oxfam, accountability also included increased collaboration and cooperation with local "partner organizations," as well as country-level Oxfam groups in planning and executing the campaign. "Together for Rights, Together against Poverty" involved the nine then-existing Oxfam national-level affiliates, "hundreds of Oxfam project partners, and thousands of Oxfam campaigners and supporters North and South."[104]

Oxfam's five-year basic rights campaign was its first attempt to have a group of Oxfams coordinate on the same issues globally at all levels. The campaign included an advocacy plan involving Oxfam partners in the South, beginning in "starter countries," Oxfam's term for countries that would participate in the campaign in collaboration

---

[100] Ibid., 39–41. [101] Ibid., 78. [102] Ibid., 78–87. [103] Ibid., 95–96.
[104] Oxfam GB, "Oxfam Launches Global Campaign," *Oxfam Campaigner* no. 16 (Autumn 1995): 1.

with domestic organizations and movements. Those countries were globally distributed and included Brazil, El Salvador, Mali, Nepal, Palestinian Occupied Territories, Pakistan, Sudan, Uganda, Vietnam, Zambia, and Zimbabwe.[105]

Tracing Oxfam's Turn to Rights

The basic rights campaign exemplifies how human rights were mobilized in service of the political realization of justice against poverty. Oxfam did not launch the kinds of appeals that AI used on behalf of individuals in its Urgent Action work, so we do not have a detailed series of appeals through which to view changes in Oxfam's language. To provide another way of observing the relative growth and change in the human rights culture of argument related to a different pursuit over a similar time frame, this section examines the language of Oxfam GB's *Annual Review* between 1975 and 2001.

The Oxfam GB *Annual Review* offers a continuous series of reports through which to observe changes and continuity in language. This annual publication is the most appropriate source for the 1975–2001 time period, since Oxfam GB staffers developed the framework of the rights-based approach that Oxfam International adopted formally in 2001. Figure 6.3 illustrates the relative frequency of mentions of rights, justice, aid, development, and poverty in the reports.[106] The reports, which were sent to rank-and-file Oxfam members, are relatively brief. The length ranges from four to twenty-one pages, with an average of sixteen pages per report. However, unlike the AI documents analyzed in the previous chapter, the Oxfam reports are not uniform in

---

[105] As listed in Oxfam GB, "Welcome to *the Big Idea*," in *The Big Idea: The Newsletter for Oxfam's New Campaign, Issue no. 1 (1994)*, MS. Oxfam CPN/8/5, folder 4 (Oxford: Oxfam, 1994), 2.

[106] Reports were coded by the author.

page size or format, and they include illustrations. These features make it difficult to standardize the reported levels of relevant terms. The reference counts reported in Figure 6.3 therefore depict a raw count, rather than standardized representation of yearly frequencies, which remains useful for comparing the emphasis placed on any given theme.

In Figure 6.3, "rights" depicts a count of any references to "basic rights" or human rights in the texts of each *Annual Review*. "Justice" denotes references to justice or injustice. The raw counts for rights and justice are represented by dots in the figure; in addition, a fitted line based on the counts approximates the general trend.[107] "Aid"

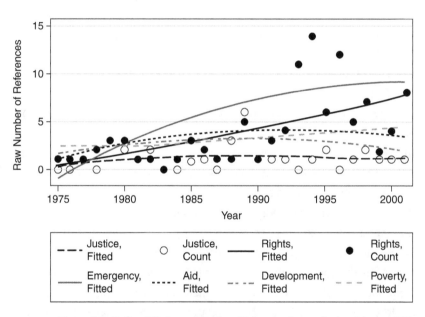

Figure 6.3 Oxfam GB *Annual Review*: Rights, justice, and other issues, 1975–2001

[107] In Figure 6.3, the fitted lines permit visualization of a summary line related to the counts of each term over time. As with the graphs in Chapter 5, the lines were generated using the Lowess statistical procedure, which estimates local weighted

denotes Oxfam's references to material transfers for purposes of aid or relief in emergencies, "development" refers to mentions of economic development, and "poverty" refers to mentions of poverty or to poor people. To make visual comparison easier, only the fitted lines for aid, development, and poverty are shown. Because the report lengths vary and later reports are somewhat longer on average, reference counts might be expected to grow overall, so the figure is best understood as a rough way to view the relative prominence of these terms over time.

As Oxfam moved toward a rights-based approach in its work against poverty, we might expect two general trends. First, there may be a fairly constant relative reliance on a justice of neighborhood, as indicated by attention to emergency and aid. The term "emergency" was used to code references to Oxfam's support for people in situations of natural disaster or famine. To provide further context, much of Oxfam's aid funding mentioned in the *Annual Reviews* was extended in situations of emergency, also characteristic of activity in the justice of neighborhood. Second, if changes are reflective of a conception of justice rooted in human rights practice, we might expect a turn to the human rights culture of argument in the 1990s as part of the political realization of justice, we should observe increasingly frequent mentions of rights.

Those trends are apparent in Figure 6.3. Notably, beginning in the late 1980s, Oxfam's references to rights, as well as attention to emergency situations, grow noticeably in comparison with the other terms. In the 1990s, rights and emergency mentions are notably more frequent than other mentions, while justice remains relatively constant, as do Oxfam's ongoing concerns related to poverty, development, and aid. Attention to the political realization of justice through rights, however, increases over time, as denoted by rights and justice mentions.

regressions based on the data points. In this particular graph, the scatterplots for emergency, aid, development, and poverty are omitted to simplify the depiction.

Notably, human rights language and justice were not entirely absent before the 1990s. On inspection of references to justice in the texts of the *Annual Reviews*, it is apparent that justice, for Oxfam, meant something broader and more generally related to social justice than AI's relatively narrow and focused use of "bring to justice," as seen in the previous chapter. For example, Oxfam GB's 1981–1982 *Annual Review* noted that, in Central America, poverty was "so often" connected with "people's search for justice and basic human rights."[108] Attention did not turn to addressing these roots through a human rights culture of argument until the next decade.

Strategic Plans for Oxfam International

Most studies that cover Oxfam's turn to rights start by referring to Oxfam International's 2001 strategic plan, without noting the background planning and preparation beforehand. Prior to that, the first strategic plan was more or less a sketch of working plans to emphasize rights in its international division. Oxfam's original ten rights were whittled down to five rights-related aims: the rights to (1) a sustainable livelihood; (2) education; (3) humanitarian protection; (4) a say (later changed to the right to be heard); and (5) gender equity. As the plan's introductory material recognized,

> We have moved over the years from transferring funds from North to South to fund projects to working with others to change the policies, practices, ideas and beliefs which cause and perpetuate poverty and suffering in our world.[109]

Beyond a "direct poverty or suffering reduction element of immediate benefit to poor women and men," it continued, Oxfam's work

---

[108] Oxfam GB, *Annual Review, 1981–82* (Oxford: Oxfam GB, 1982), 3.

[109] Oxfam International, "International Division, Strategic Plan 1999–2004" (Oxfam Archives, folder MS. Oxfam PRG/2/1/1, circa 1995), 2.

has to support people's efforts to build their own capacity to overcome poverty or suffering now and in the future ... [I]n all cases we and our partners must be trying to address the underlying causes.[110]

The archives show that Oxfam GB carried out a complex effort prior to the strategic planning efforts, to draft rights-based "strategic change objectives" for Oxfam's work in the field, through a process that sought input from Oxfam's in-country workers. Upon unification, the national Oxfams would situate their work in relation to the 2001 strategic plan, entitled *Towards Global Equity*.[111]

The second strategic plan became the vehicle for implementing the rights-based approach worldwide, and it begins by reproducing a statement of Oxfam International's mission, which had been adopted in 1996. The mission statement begins by framing poverty as an "injustice" and asserting that

> Basic human needs and rights can be met. These include the rights to a sustainable livelihood, and the rights and capacities to participate in societies and make positive changes to people's lives.[112]

The statement further asserts that Oxfam's "ultimate goal is to enable people to exercise their rights and manage their own lives," and that,

> for people to be able to exercise their rights: (a) opportunities must be created so people can participate in governing all aspects of their lives, and (b) they must have the genuine capacity to organize and take advantage of those opportunities.[113]

---

[110] Ibid. [111] Oxfam International, *Towards Global Equity*.

[112] Oxfam International, "Oxfam International's Mission," adopted by the Board of Oxfam International, Ottawa 1996, item 2, cited in Oxfam International, *Towards Global Equity*, https://web.archive.org/web/20050202203946/http:/www.oxfam.org/eng/pdfs/strat_plan.pdf.

[113] Ibid., items 7 and 8.

More Cross-fertilization in the Search for Justice

This chapter has thus far emphasized the emergence of a rights-based approach within Oxfam GB, as an example of the broader relevance of human rights practice to justice-seeking. Oxfam GB's groundwork on basic rights was translated to Oxfam International and other Oxfams. Further, the movement of staff between human rights organizations, private foundations, government, and other kinds of NGOs maintained a fertile ground for rights-based ideas to take root in the development sector.

Experiences of key staff members who were acting in the context in Latin America, and also Asia, played a strong role in orienting Oxfam toward human rights. When Ray Offenheiser assumed leadership of Oxfam America, the US branch of Oxfam, in November 1995, he became involved not only in recasting Oxfam America's programming but also in supporting and advocating for a rights-based approach as plans were made for its full adoption within Oxfam International.[114]

Offenheiser had done graduate work in tropical agriculture at Cornell University, and been exposed to human rights ideas as a participant in the Chile solidarity movement as a student. His technical expertise and his interest in human rights and social change landed him in professional roles first at the Inter-American Foundation and then at the Ford Foundation. While at Ford, Offenheiser had worked as a regional funder in Peru and in Chile, and then had moved to do similar work in Asia as Ford's country representative in Bangladesh.[115] The Ford Foundation provided significant global programmatic support for human rights at that time.[116]

---

[114] Offenheiser, June 13 and 17, 2019. [115] Ibid.

[116] Peter D. Bell, "The Ford Foundation as a Transnational Actor," *International Organization* 25, no. 3 (1971): 465–478; Wendy H. Wong, Ron Levi, and Julia Deutsch, "Domesticating the Field: The Ford Foundation and the Development of International Human Rights," in *Professional Networks in Transnational Governance*, eds. Leonard Seabrooke and Lasse Folke Henriksen (Cambridge: Cambridge University Press, 2017), 82–100.

By the time Offenheiser was recruited by Oxfam America, the decision to confederate the Oxfams had been made. Offenheiser was drawn to the prospect of shaping Oxfam's global work and saw human rights as core guiding principles. He pushed inside the organization for use of a rights-based approach as a way to unify and globalize the work of Oxfam.[117] Offenheiser had a bird's-eye perspective on the human rights movement, as well as familiarity with the field of global development, and was also a forceful voice for a human rights approach in discussions with other global NGOs.[118] Offenheiser's approach to organizational leadership was one that emphasized learning and effectiveness. He recounted his views that that the grassroots funding approach that Oxfam America had favored in the past – one consistent with the justice of neighborhood – could be more effective *and* more relevant to what was happening on the ground. Echoing Feeney, Offenheiser noted that "field people understood the need for rights."[119]

Conclusion

Rights-related action to support populations in need marked a notable shift in development groups' approaches to justice-seeking. In one author's words, this approach also indicates

> a changing paradigm of justice that is less legal and more social – which moves part of the discourse on human rights from the courtrooms and the top-institutions to areas where there is a dire need for protection of human rights.[120]

For the development sector, a rights-based approach to poverty was a step away from a needs-based or welfarist approach

---

[117] Offenheiser, June 13 and 17, 2019; see also Esther Scott, *Oxfam America: Becoming a Global Campaigning Organization* (Cambridge, MA: Harvard Kennedy School, 2004).
[118] Dorsey, July 2, 2018. [119] Offenheiser, June 13 and 17, 2019.
[120] Sano, "Development and Human Rights," 752.

and toward enhancing the participation and empowerment of the people that development groups hoped to serve. Empowerment involved supporting poor people's capacity to hold their own governments accountable. Calling upon rights also lent a gravity and urgency to the problem of poverty, because it emphasized universal human equality and questioned why and how some people were systematically deprived of the rights to subsistence and security that are basic to a life of dignity. Attention to political rights, then, could be seen as an untapped resource for economic and social development. Oxfam turned toward human rights as a lever in the pursuit of social justice by tailoring the use of rights to work against poverty.

The example of Oxfam demonstrates how the culture of argument developed by the human rights movement transferred to efforts toward the political realization of justice on development and poverty concerns. The trajectories of Feeney and Offenheiser showed how their experiences related to encounters with injustice in their work caused them to see the political prominence of human rights norms at the global level as a basis for advocating political representation of people experiencing poverty and economic injustice. The most dramatic shift prompted by rights-based approaches to development was the appeal to human rights to cast the demands of social justice as matters that require political realization. Oxfam used civil and political rights in its arguments, however, but also began to integrate rights language with social justice advocacy.

Viewing this case in comparison with how the human rights movement used its own tools of justice also demonstrates the value of cross-sector comparison. The seeming limitations of human rights approaches for economic justice, and broader social justice, did not stop Oxfam from choosing human rights as a path for seeking more justice. Human rights NGOs are now broadening their justice goals, although the integration of civil and political human rights with economic, social, and cultural human rights in the pursuit of social justice is not fully fledged.

7

Conclusion

Human rights practices have embedded elements of justice into global politics. By viewing human rights innovations through a justice lens, I have sought to show how global human rights came to constitute a language of justice. To give form and content to a lofty concept, I have focused on individuals and their work within two major nongovernmental organizations (NGOs). The result is a human rights–informed conception of justice: the expansion of neighborhood through the persistent use of transnational appeals; the creation of a new culture of argument by uniting international legal norms with continued expression of concern for individuals; and efforts to address structural inequality by bringing rights to bear on social and economic injustice. The emergence and application of rights as tools for justice is only part of the story. Notably, the case studies show that changes in human rights practices have emerged in response to the demands of justice.

The case studies of Amnesty International's (AI's) Urgent Action (UA) initiative and Oxfam's basic rights framework demonstrate the underlying presence of active care – a disposition of care informed by skill, awareness, and connection – as advocates used human rights tools to come to terms with injustice. The words of people in previous chapters communicate their recognition that engaged action was required to meet the challenges. They refer to observing patterns of repression that "we saw subsequently, all over the place" (Tracy Ulltveit-Moe, AI's International Secretariat); being "willing to be on call ... if London can get information" (Scott Harrison, Amnesty International USA UA Office); and connecting organizational policies to the persons most affected, as "field people understood the need for rights" (Ray Offenheiser, Oxfam America).

The emergence of human rights practice depended in part on global advocates who chose to take action as active bystanders, or "upstanders," rather than persons affected directly by injustice.[1] For that reason, I have also queried the ways in which, once the global neighborhood is expanded, activists are themselves further challenged to acquire more complete understandings of injustice in local contexts. The justice of neighborhood's active care requires moving beyond compassion to equal recognition of the global neighbor. Active care also requires seeking adequate understanding, recognition, and informed judgment in light of the potential partiality of one's own view. Taking another's part responsibly, as Brooke Ackerly has argued, requires not only "conscientious activists" who are willing to engage with injustice but "connected activists" who maintain networks of informed solidarity in relation with other advocates and with those whose rights are most at risk.[2]

Changing understandings of the demands of justice continue to stimulate innovations in human rights practice. The features of justice employed in the previous chapters as theoretical lenses on human rights – the expansion of neighborhood, the political realization of justice, and the integration of social justice – are dynamic. These processes have worked themselves out in a rough sequence with relation to one another. The sequence is also additive. Political tools furnished by law and a human rights culture of argument are supported

---

[1] On active bystanders, see Ervin Staub, "Preventing Violence and Promoting Active Bystandership and Peace: My Life in Research and Applications," *Peace and Conflict: Journal of Peace Psychology* 24, no. 1 (2018): 95–111. On upstanders, see Martha Minow, *Upstanders, Whistle-Blowers, and Rescuers*, Koningsberger Lecture, delivered on December 13, 2014, University of Utrecht (The Hague: Eleven International Publishing, 2016).

[2] Ackerly, *Just Responsibility*.

and sustained by active care and habits that are part of a justice of neighborhood. The challenges for the integration of social and economic justice concerns into law and politics are significant, but the view that social justice belongs in the human rights universe has prompted new conceptions of how human rights should be configured in international law and politics. Law is not the full answer to structures of injustice, particularly because legal institutions can themselves perpetuate injustice, but the skillful articulation and application of law can create a structure of remedy that supports affected persons' own agency.

The view presented here of the incremental nature of human rights work necessarily relies on an incremental view of how justice may be achieved. Unfortunately, technologies of human rights violations do not stand still, a fact that calls for continuing awareness and innovation in applied justice advocacy.[3] Nevertheless, a view of human rights practice as an evolving form of justice work inspires optimism. The case studies show that human rights as a language of justice still has the capacity for growth. The language of human rights has been adapted and applied over time in ways that respond to contingent political circumstances that challenge prevailing approaches. Action for human rights and ideas about justice, in this view, have become mutually constitutive.

The optimism I refer to stems not from belief in the human rights framework in and of itself. A perspective on the human rights movement as something akin to a faith commitment features strongly in critiques of the human rights movement and of AI in particular.[4] On

---

[3] For a balanced collection of essays on the challenges posed by technology, see Molly K. Land and Jay D. Aronson, eds., *New Technologies for Human Rights Law and Practice* (Cambridge: Cambridge University Press, 2018). On technology and justice, see Molly K. Land and Jay D. Aronson, "Human Rights and Technology: New Challenges for Justice and Accountability," *Annual Review of Law and Social Science* 16 (2020): 223–240.

[4] See Moyn, *Not Enough*; Hopgood, *Keepers of the Flame*.

the contrary, what I observe in the practice of human rights is a commitment to application of the skills and habits of justice-seeking. Nor does optimism stem solely from the inspiring stories included here of how individual people can persevere and innovate in the pursuit of justice. Optimism is warranted because the human rights struggles preceding and occupying the current moment have established a foothold for justice that is likely a permanent feature of the international system. Human rights advocates have been able to influence national and international practices across national borders.[5] Still, it seems to be the success rather than the failure of the human rights framework that has also prompted arguments that human rights proponents should be more attentive to embedding human rights in national and local mass politics.[6] Here I reflect briefly on the implications of the notion that human rights practice has become a language of justice in the world.

Human rights remain a rich resource for the practical pursuit of justice within the international system. Early human rights actors, as well as development groups, cited human rights as reasons for concrete extensions of concern intended to alleviate human suffering. Just as David Forsythe has said in his study of the International Committee of the Red Cross, for human rights actors, "the moral imperative led law,

---

[5] Thomas Risse, Stephen C. Ropp, and Kathryn Sikkink, eds., *The Power of Human Rights: International Norms and Domestic Change* (Cambridge: Cambridge University Press, 1999); Thomas Risse, Steven C. Ropp, and Kathryn Sikkink, eds., *The Persistent Power of Human Rights: From Commitment to Compliance* (Cambridge: Cambridge University Press, 2013); Christian Reus-Smit, *Individual Rights and the Making of the International System* (Cambridge: Cambridge University Press, 2013).

[6] For a critical but sympathetic view of political shortcomings of human rights NGOs with regard to national politics, see Jack Snyder, "Empowering Rights through Mass Movements, Religion, and Reform Parties," in *Human Rights Futures*, eds. Stephen Hopgood, Jack Snyder, and Leslie Vinjamuri (Cambridge: Cambridge University Press, 2017), 88–113.

not the other way around ... Law was to facilitate and ensure the repetition of the practical action that had already occurred."[7] The first contribution of human rights practice to justice, the expansion of the global neighborhood, produced a form of transnational politics set into motion by members of civil society who reached beyond the borders of their own countries. In this respect, the human rights action character- istic of the justice of neighborhood has an affinity with humanitarian work. It need not originate with the nation-state.[8] But what about international politics among states?

In standard academic usage, "international relations" refers in the first instance to politics among states. In contrast, I have empha- sized efforts of individuals and NGOs to affect global, national, and local politics. As the discussion of AI's Urgent Action network makes clear, the justice of neighborhood entailed a direct transnational response by individuals to human rights abuses: harm perpetrated by nation-states as political actors in the pursuit of power. Through human rights practice, the ambition to stop repression through direct activism began to speak to international politics.

The early practice of human rights quickly kindled the legal imagination, as activists' habits of response confronted the political causes of rights violations. Today, human rights work is a huge and varied enterprise, with a great deal of formal infrastructure, but it took a leap of imagination for activists to believe that they could coordinate transnational work for individuals to stop human rights violations. It took a second leap to bring that work to political fruition. The path to human rights as the political realization of justice, the second component of justice I have examined, also focuses

---

[7] Forsythe, *The Humanitarians*, 30.

[8] Alison Brysk has demonstrated how human rights considerations have motivated many nation-states' foreign policy; see *Global Good Samaritans: Human Rights as Foreign Policy* (Oxford: Oxford University Press, 2009).

heavily not on engagements between nation-states but on how human rights advocacy engages with state power. Chapter 5 demonstrated how an emerging human rights culture of argument allowed UA appeals to speak the language of justice by invoking both care and law. Through law, human rights practice has secured necessary international procedures, standards, and arguments for pursuing legal justice. A sense of justice related to international politics is now bolstered and reinforced by human rights provisions in law and intergovernmental institutions, and not only by human rights' status as a language of justice. As shown in Chapter 6, human rights language has changed international politics by furnishing a medium for justice-related protections at the international level that have also been invoked by NGOs in the development sector. Nevertheless, scholars, activists, and observers continue to point out the shortcomings of human rights practice with regard to the integration of economic and social justice concerns.

In AI's appeals directed at nation-states, as well the extension of rights arguments to inform Oxfam's action for economic justice, human rights practice has swung the fulcrum of justice fulfillment away from the charity of neighbors to the proper recognition of the political agency of affected persons. Oxfam, already skilled in implementing the justice of neighborhood, was drawn in the 1990s to human rights because they incorporate political demands. The case studies of the language in UA alerts, and of Oxfam's turn to rights, document the ways in which human rights language has enabled new forms of argument that can be used as levers of influence by civil society actors within the domestic politics of nation-states and in international organizations. Human rights norms as law have institutionalized new expectations of state behavior that, although they do not replace the language of power, pose a counterpoint to it that facilitates the pursuit of justice on international terrain.

As a vehicle for social change, human rights has become a powerful discourse, but some critics also see a downside of rights talk as a discourse of power in international politics. These two features of human rights language can be situated in opposition, but they need not be.

As leading human rights NGOs have become more authoritative, their positioning in the human rights universe may constrain their modes of action, making them less willing to be bold, and more comfortable with status quo politics.[9] Their established reputations, their power as gatekeepers, and their capacity in comparison to smaller NGOs bolster their authority.[10] In addition, critical scholars point out that a human rights frame privileges classical liberal, individualist views originating in the wealthy Global North while expressing wariness of the potential to reproduce social relations that contributed to the structural injustices of colonialism, racism, and gender bias.[11] For similar reasons, others have critiqued development policies touting aid ownership and stakeholder participation.[12] Each of the critiques just mentioned points to an imperfect fit between rights and justice that merits recognition and remedy.

The changes in human rights practice over time, seen in light of demands of justice, suggest that human rights practice should not be seen as a static reflection of what is possible.[13] The human rights

---

[9] Stroup and Wong, *The Authority Trap*.

[10] Carpenter, *Lost Causes*; Clifford Bob, *The Marketing of Rebellion: Insurgents, Media, and International Activism* (Cambridge: Cambridge University Press, 2005).

[11] See Julia Suárez-Krabbe, "Democratising Democracy, Humanising Human Rights: European Decolonial Social Movements and the 'Alternative Thinking of Alternatives,'" *Migration Letters* 10, no. 3 (2013): 333–341; Suárez-Krabbe, "The Other Side of the Story."

[12] T. D. Harper-Shipman, *Rethinking Ownership of Development in Africa* (Abingdon: Routledge, 2010); Hertel, *Tethered Fates*.

[13] For a compelling test of possible problems with the prevalence of human rights law as related to economic and social justice concerns, see Beth A. Simmons and Anton Strezhnev, "Human Rights and Human Welfare: Looking for a 'Dark Side' to International Law," in *Human Rights Futures*, 60–87.

framework as a path to justice may at some point reach its limits, but human rights possess two unique features that, to some extent, keep human rights practices from losing their edge as tools of justice. The first feature is that the users of human rights tools become subject to critique from the very standpoint of human rights that they propound, and their legitimacy depends on how well they respond to those critiques. As Allen Buchanan has noted, "the very concept of human rights itself contains resources for correcting biases in its interpretation."[14] Human rights is hardly a self-correcting practice, but its tools render unjust consequences of the practice more visible.

The second feature is the malleability of human rights practice, despite the level of institutionalization in law and international organization. Even where tailored protections in international human rights law are incomplete, local, regional, and global activists use human rights in new and uncharted ways. As the case study of Oxfam showed, human rights ideas and mobilizing strategies are useful tools for advocacy on issues beyond civil and political rights. Research by Jackie Smith documents how people are "bringing human rights home," by using rights as guidelines for city governance in the USA, for example.[15] Patterns of networked activism exhibit changes in structure and scale such that, although nation-states have not ceased to impose limits on NGOs' activities, actors on a wide range of global and local issues no longer limit themselves to a reactive approach to the nation-state, nor are they dependent on leadership from northern NGOs.[16]

---

[14] Allen E. Buchanan, *Justice, Legitimacy, and Self-determination: Moral Foundations for International Law* (Oxford: Oxford University Press, 2004), 121.

[15] Jackie Smith, "Responding to Globalization and Urban Conflict: Human Rights City Initiatives," *Studies in Social Justice* 11, no. 2 (2017): 347–368.

[16] Christopher L. Pallas and Elizabeth A. Bloodgood, eds., *Beyond the Boomerang: New Patterns in Transcalar Advocacy* (Tuscaloosa: University of Alabama Press, forthcoming), 121.

Many expressions of justice concerns draw on the language of human rights: environmental justice, racial justice, indigenous rights, LGBTQI rights, gender equity, and economic and social justice concerns. The variation illustrates the broad applicability of human rights as tools of justice. Even where such issues are incompletely recognized in international human rights law, people acting for a broad variety of concerns are being protected under the language of "human rights defenders," based on the 1998 UN declaration widely referred to by its nickname, the UN Declaration on Human Rights Defenders.[17] In 2020, Mary Lawlor, the UN's Special Rapporteur on the Situation of Human Rights Defenders, singled out rights defenders in the following areas as "the most marginalized and vulnerable":

> women defenders, those defending the rights of lesbian, gay, bisexual, transgender and intersex persons, defenders who are children, defenders with disabilities, defenders working on the rights of migrants and related issues, those working on the climate crisis and defenders working in isolated and remote areas.[18]

Because human rights as a language of justice is so versatile, we can observe local activists adapting human rights language for their own purposes.[19] As Alison Brysk writes, "human rights is movement."[20] Activists adapt and interpret human rights at home and abroad.[21]

---

[17] "Declaration on the Right and Responsibility of Individuals, Groups and Organs of Society to Promote and Protect Universally Recognized Human Rights and Fundamental Freedoms."

[18] UN Special Rapporteur on the Situation of Human Rights Defenders, Mary Lawlor, "Summary," Report on the Priorities of the Mandate of Special Rapporteur to the General Assembly at Its 75th Session (July 16, 2020), UN document no. A/75/165, www.ohchr.org/EN/Issues/SRHRDefenders/Pages/priorities-sr.aspx.

[19] Smith, "Domesticating International Human Rights Norms"; Hertel, "Re-framing Human Rights Advocacy."

[20] Alison Brysk, *The Future of Human Rights* (Cambridge: Polity Press, 2018).

[21] Hertel, "Re-framing Human Rights Advocacy."

Locally situated activists make new claims that both call upon and stretch human rights concepts, testing the conventionally recognized limits of rights talk. This is a testament to the vitality of the human rights culture of argument.

Finally, as justice advocates, human rights NGOs and other actors are themselves subject to the standards of justice. NGOs are nonideal agents of justice. Global NGOs are often external to the circumstances that they aim to affect, which can offer points of leverage but also engender inequality. As recognized at the outset, many global activists have engaged in human rights practice from a position of relative privilege and safety. North–South encounters among NGOs have pushed the older and better established, usually Northern, organizations in the rights and development sectors to be more responsive to within-sector global power differentials and differences of perspective. Such dynamics are ongoing in the human rights movement and other movements at the global and national levels.[22]

To paraphrase Beitz, human rights may be the closest thing we have to a common language of justice in global politics.[23] Human rights practice has changed the terms of engagement in global politics by providing a common standard for the normative evaluation of political realities. The human rights culture of argument now operates against a background of institutionalized monitoring procedures in intergovernmental organizations. In addition, human rights language has become a medium for justice-related claims people make of their governments. Even with these developments, however, it is a mistake to see human rights as a finished project. Economic, social, and cultural rights have yet to be fully supplied with dedicated human rights tools at

---

[22] For a comparative study of how movements in three national contexts have negotiated solidarity, see Rachel L. Einwohner, Kaitlin Kelly-Thompson, Valeria Sinclair-Chapman, et al., "Active Solidarity: Intersectional Solidarity in Action," *Social Politics* 28(3) (2021), online first: https://doi.org/10.1093/sp/jxz052.

[23] See Beitz, "Human Rights as a Common Concern" as discussed in Chapter 2.

the global level. Still, extrapolation from the aforementioned examples of newer local activism, and from the ingenuity that early rights actors demonstrated, should cause us to expect further development of human rights arguments with regard to broader justice concerns in politics.

Human rights advocacy brings people face to face with the incomplete achievement of justice: with implications for the limitations of the work, how the practice could be improved, and ways that the process itself can be more just. Productive tension between human rights actors' sense of justice and recognition of the ways in which justice is not yet fulfilled continue to propel human rights work. Such tension is a source of learning and innovation.

The strength of human rights as a path to justice lies in its ability to draw attention to the conduct of international, national, and local politics as it impacts human lives and livelihoods. Human rights practice has accommodated and supported diverse forms of appeal even while recognizing that in the face of power, human rights arguments take place within a discourse of unequals. Although state and corporate power exceed the power of individuals as bearers of rights, human rights as a justice practice has enlarged the scope of justice claims and broadened who has standing to appeal for justice in international politics. As demands of justice, human rights can be taken up by anyone in the global neighborhood.

Abouharb, M. Rodwan, and David Cingranelli. *Human Rights and Structural Adjustment*. Cambridge: Cambridge University Press, 2007.

Ackerly, Brooke A. *Just Responsibility: A Human Rights Theory of Global Justice*. Oxford: Oxford University Press, 2018.

Adler, Emanuel, and Vincent Pouliot. "International Practices." *International Theory* 3, no. 1 (2011): 1–36.

Adler, Emanuel, and Vincent Pouliot. *International Practices*. Cambridge: Cambridge University Press, 2011.

Ako, Matilda Aberese, Nana Akua Anyidoho, and Gordon Crawford. "NGOs, Rights-Based Approaches and the Potential for Progressive Development in Local Contexts: Constraints and Challenges in Northern Ghana." *Journal of Human Rights Practice* 5, no. 1 (2013): 46–74.

Alston, Philip. "Ships Passing in the Night: The Current State of the Human Rights and Development Debate Seen through the Lens of the Millennium Development Goals." *Human Rights Quarterly* 27, no. 3 (2005): 755–829.

Amnesty International. "AI@50: The Amnesty International Timeline." London: Amnesty International (2011). http://static.amnesty.org/ai50/ai50-amnesty-international-timeline.pdf.

Amnesty International. "Amnesty International Impact Report: 2012–2013." Amnesty International Secretariat, AI Index no. ORG 30/009/201 (October 2014). www.amnesty.org/download/Documents/8000/org300092014en.pdf.

Amnesty International. "Brazil." In *Annual Report 1972–73*, 46–47. London: Amnesty International Publications, 1973.

Amnesty International. "Education: OxfAMnesty Activists Join Forces for Women's Rights – Belgium" (2013). www.amnesty.org/en/latest/education/2013/09/oxfamnesty-activists-join-forces-for-womens-rights-belgium/.

Amnesty International. "International Executive Committee, Meeting in Utrecht, 6–7 September 1972. Agenda Item 9," Amsterdam: International Institute for the Study of Social History, Amnesty International, International Secretariat Archives. Document location: ARCH00200, Inv. No. 51, Folder 51, 1972.

Amnesty International. *Report on Allegations of Torture in Brazil.* London: Amnesty International Publications, 1972.

Amnesty International. *Report on Torture.* London: Duckworth, in association with Amnesty International Publications, 1973.

Amnesty International. "Review of the Urgent Action Campaigning Tool: Report of the Surveys to Sections and IS Staff." Amnesty International Secretariat, AI index no: ACT 60/5668/2017 (internal) (February 2017).

Amnesty International. "Urgent Actions Visualised." Amnesty International, International Secretariat (2021). https://decoders.amnesty.org/projects/dec ode-urgent-actions/results.

Amnesty International UK. "Pocket Protest." (2021). www.amnesty.org.uk/iss ues/pocket-protest.

Amnesty International USA. "Joan Baez: A Lifetime of Human Rights Advocacy." (2019). www.amnestyusa.org/joan-baez-a-lifetime-of-human-rights-advocacy/.

Amnesty International USA. "Urgent Action: Disappeared during Covid-19 Quarantine (Argentina UA 120/20)." (2020). www.amnestyusa.org/urgent-actions/urgent-action-disappeared-during-covid-19-quarantine-argentina-ua-120-20/.

Anonymous, "Joan Baez Heads Benefit," *San Francisco Examiner*, May 23, 1974.

"Appeal." In *The Concise Oxford Dictionary*, edited by J. B. Sykes. Oxford: Oxford University Press, 1982.

Arquidiocese de São Paulo [Archdiocese of São Paulo]. *Projeto "Brasil: Nunca Mais."* São Paulo: Arquidiocese de São Paulo, 1985. http://bnmdigital.mp f.mp.br/pt-br/.

Baehr, Peter R. "Amnesty International and Its Self-imposed Limited Mandate." *Netherlands Quarterly of Human Rights* 12, no. 1 (1994): 5–21.

Barnett, Michael. *Empire of Humanity: A History of Humanitarianism.* Ithaca, NY: Cornell University Press, 2011.

Barton, Amy, Paul Bracke, and Ann Marie Clark. "Digitization, Data Curation, and Political Science Research: The Amnesty International Urgent Action Bulletins Project." *IASSIST Quarterly* 40, no. 1 (2016): 28–35.

Beaumont, Peter. "Oxfam to Close in 18 Countries and Cut 1,500 Staff Amid Coronavirus Pressures." *The Guardian*, May 20, 2020.

Beitz, Charles. "Human Rights as a Common Concern." *American Political Science Review* 95, no. 2 (2001): 269–282.

Beitz, Charles R. *The Idea of Human Rights*. Oxford: Oxford University Press, 2009.

Beitz, Charles R., and Robert E. Goodin. *Global Basic Rights*. Oxford: Oxford University Press, 2009.

Beitz, Charles R., and Robert E. Goodin. "Introduction: Basic Rights and Beyond." In *Global Basic Rights*, edited by Charles R. Beitz and Robert E. Goodin, 1–24. Oxford: Oxford University Press, 2009.

Bell, Peter D. "The Ford Foundation as a Transnational Actor." *International Organization* 25, no. 3 (1971): 465–478.

Benenson, Peter. "The Forgotten Prisoners." *The Observer*, May 28, 1961, 20.

Benhabib, Seyla, Jeremy Waldron, Bonnie Honig, Will Kymlicka, and Robert Post. *Another Cosmopolitanism*. The Berkeley Tanner Lectures. Oxford; New York: Oxford University Press, 2006.

Bevernage, Berber. *History, Memory, and State-Sponsored Violence: Time and Justice*. New York: Routledge, 2012.

Black, Maggie. *Oxfam: The First Fifty Years*. Oxford: Oxfam, 1992.

Bob, Clifford. *The Marketing of Rebellion: Insurgents, Media, and International Activism*. Cambridge: Cambridge University Press, 2005.

Brazil Comissão Nacional da Verdade (CNV) [National Truth Commission]. *Relatório da Comissão Nacional da Verdade*. Brasilia: CNV, 2014. http://cnv.memoriasreveladas.gov.br/images/pdf/relatorio/vo lume_1_digital.pdf.

Brysk, Alison. *The Future of Human Rights*. Cambridge: Polity Press, 2018.

Brysk, Alison. *Global Good Samaritans: Human Rights as Foreign Policy*. Oxford: Oxford University Press, 2009.

Buchanan, Allen E. *The Heart of Human Rights*. Oxford: Oxford University Press, 2013.

Buchanan, Allen E. *Justice, Legitimacy, and Self-determination: Moral Foundations for International Law.* Oxford: Oxford University Press, 2004.

Buchanan, Tom. *Amnesty International and Human Rights Activism in Postwar Britain, 1945–1977.* Cambridge: Cambridge University Press, 2020.

Buchanan, Tom. "'The Truth Will Set You Free': The Making of Amnesty International." *Journal of Contemporary History* 37, no. 4 (2002): 575–597.

Campbell, Tom. "Justice." In *The New Oxford Companion to Law,* online, edited by Peter Cane, Joanne Conaghan, and David M. Walker. Oxford: Oxford University Press, 2008.

Carella, Anna, and Brooke Ackerly. "Ignoring Rights Is Wrong: Re-politicizing Gender Equality and Development with the Rights-Based Approach." *International Feminist Journal of Politics* 19, no. 2 (2017): 137–152.

Carpenter, Daniel, and Colin D. Moore. "When Canvassers Became Activists: Antislavery Petitioning and the Political Mobilization of American Women." *American Political Science Review* 108, no. 3 (2014): 479–498.

Carpenter, R. Charli. *Lost Causes: Agenda Vetting in Global Issue Networks and the Shaping of Human Security.* Ithaca, NY: Cornell University Press, 2016.

Chong, Daniel P. L. *Freedom from Poverty: NGOs and Human Rights Praxis.* Philadelphia: University of Pennsylvania Press, 2011.

Clark, Ann Marie. *Diplomacy of Conscience: Amnesty International and Changing International Human Rights Norms.* Princeton, NJ: Princeton University Press, 2001.

Clark, Ann Marie. "What Kind of Justice for Human Rights?" In *Human Rights and Justice: Philosophical, Economic, and Social Perspectives,* edited by Melissa Labonte and Kurt Mills, 14–32. Abingdon-on-Thames: Routledge, 2018.

Clark, Ann Marie, Elisabeth J. Friedman, and Kathryn Hochstetler. "The Sovereign Limits of Global Civil Society: A Comparison of NGO Participation in UN World Conferences on the Environment, Human Rights, and Women." *World Politics* 51, no. 1 (1998): 1–35.

Clark, Ann Marie, and Kathryn Sikkink. "Information Effects and Human Rights Data: Is the Good News About Increased Human Rights Information Bad News for Human Rights Measures?" *Human Rights Quarterly* 35, no. 3 (2013): 539–568.

Clark, Ann Marie, and Bi Zhao. "'Who Did What for Whom?' Amnesty International's Urgent Actions as Activist-Generated Data." *Journal of Human Rights* 19, no. 1 (2020): 46–66.

Cornwall, Andrea, and Celestine Nyamu-Musembi. "Putting the 'Rights-Based Approach' to Development into Perspective." *Third World Quarterly* 25, no. 8 (2004): 1415–1437.

Dancy, Geoff. "Human Rights Pragmatism: Belief, Inquiry, and Action." *European Journal of International Relations* 22, no. 3 (2016): 512–535.

Dancy, Geoff, and Christopher Fariss. "The Heavens Are Always Fallen: A Neo-constitutive Approach to Human Rights in Global Society." *Law and Contemporary Problems* 81, no. 4 (2018): 73–100.

Dancy, Geoff, Bridget E. Marchesi, Tricia D. Olsen, et al. "Behind Bars and Bargains: New Findings on Transitional Justice in Emerging Democracies." *International Studies Quarterly* 63, no. 1 (2019): 99–110.

Dancy, Geoff, and Verónica Michel. "Human Rights Enforcement from Below: Private Actors and Prosecutorial Momentum in Latin America and Europe." *International Studies Quarterly* 60, no. 1 (2016): 173–188.

Donnelly, Jack. "Human Rights." In *The Oxford Handbook of Political Theory*, edited by John S. Dryzek, Bonnie Honig, and Anne Phillips, 601–620. Oxford: Oxford University Press, 2006.

Dorsey, Ellen. "The Global Women's Movement: Articulating a New Vision of Global Governance." In *The Politics of Global Governance: International Organizations in an Interdependent World*, edited by Paul F. Diehl, 436–461. Boulder, CO: Lynne Rienner Publishers, 2001.

Dunn, Kevin C., and Iver B. Neumann. *Undertaking Discourse Analysis for Social Research*. Ann Arbor: University of Michigan Press, 2016.

Eade, Deborah, Suzanne Williams, and Oxfam. *The Oxfam Handbook of Development and Relief*. Three vols. Oxford: Oxfam, 1995.

Einwohner, Rachel L., Kaitlin Kelly-Thompson, Valeria Sinclair-Chapman, Fernando Tormos-Aponte, S. Laurel Weldon, Jared M. Wright, Charles Wu. "Active Solidarity: Intersectional Solidarity in Action." *Social Politics* 28(3) (2021). Online first: https://doi.org/10.1093/sp/jxz052.

Finnemore, Martha, and Kathryn Sikkink. "International Norm Dynamics and Political Change." *International Organization* 52, no. 4 (1998): 887–917.

Forsythe, David P. *The Humanitarians: The International Committee of the Red Cross.* New York: Cambridge University Press, 2005.

Fregoso, Rosa Linda. "'We Want Them Alive!': The Politics and Culture of Human Rights." *Social Identities* 12, no. 2 (2006): 109–138.

Friedman, Elisabeth Jay. "Gendering the Agenda: The Impact of the Transnational Women's Rights Movement at the UN Conferences of the 1990s." *Women's Studies International Forum* 26, no. 4 (2003): 313–331.

Friedman, Elisabeth Jay, Kathryn Hochstetler, and Ann Marie Clark. *Sovereignty, Democracy, and Global Civil Society: State-Society Relations at UN World Conferences.* Albany: State University of New York Press, 2005.

Frost, Mervyn, and Silviya Lechner. "Understanding International Practices from the Internal Point of View." *Journal of International Political Theory* 12, no. 3 (2015): 299–319.

Fukuda-Parr, Sakiko. "International Obligations for Economic and Social Rights: The Case of the Millennium Development Goal Eight." In *Economic Rights: Conceptual, Measurement, and Policy Issues*, edited by Shareen Hertel and Lanse Minkler, 284–309. New York: Cambridge University Press, 2007.

Goering, Curt. "Amnesty International and Economic, Social, and Cultural Rights." In *Ethics in Action: The Ethical Challenges of International Human Rights Organizations*, edited by Daniel Bell and Jean-Marc Coicaud, 204–217. Cambridge: Cambridge University Press, 2007.

Goodhart, Michael E. *Injustice: Political Theory for the Real World.* Oxford: Oxford University Press, 2018.

Gready, Paul. "Organisational Theories of Change in the Era of Organisational Cosmopolitanism: Lessons from ActionAid's Human Rights-Based Approach." *Third World Quarterly* 34, no. 8 (2013): 1339–1360.

Green, Duncan, and Anna Macdonald. "Power and Change: The Arms Trade Treaty." Oxford: Oxfam GB for Oxfam International, 2015. https://oxfamili brary.openrepository.com/bitstream/handle/10546/338471/cs-arms-trade-treaty-160115-en.pdf?sequence=1&isAllowed=y.

Guest, Iain. *Behind the Disappearances.* Philadelphia: University of Pennsylvania Press, 1992.

Harper-Shipman, T. D. *Rethinking Ownership of Development in Africa.* Abingdon: Routledge, 2010.

Hendrix, Cullen S., and Wendy H. Wong. "When Is the Pen Truly Mighty? Regime Type and the Efficacy of Naming and Shaming in Curbing Human Rights Abuses." *British Journal of Political Science* 43, no. 3 (2013): 651–672.

Hertel, Shareen. "Re-framing Human Rights Advocacy: The Rise of Economic Rights." In *Human Rights Futures*, edited by Stephen Hopgood, Jack Snyder, and Leslie Vinjamuri, 237–260. Cambridge: Cambridge University Press, 2017.

Hertel, Shareen. *Tethered Fates: Companies, Communities, and Rights at Stake.* Oxford: Oxford University Press, 2019.

Hertel, Shareen. *Unexpected Power: Conflict and Change among Transnational Activists.* Ithaca, NY: Cornell University Press, 2006.

Honig, Bonnie. *Emergency Politics: Paradox, Law, Democracy.* Princeton, NJ: Princeton University Press, 2009.

Hopgood, Stephen. *Keepers of the Flame: Understanding Amnesty International.* Ithaca, NY: Cornell University Press, 2006.

Hopgood, Stephen, Jack Snyder, and Leslie Vinjamuri, eds. *Human Rights Futures.* Cambridge: Cambridge University Press, 2017.

Howard-Hassmann, Rhoda. *In Defense of Universal Human Rights.* Cambridge: Polity Press, 2019.

Htun, Mala, and S. Laurel Weldon. *The Logics of Gender Justice: State Action on Women's Rights around the World.* Cambridge: Cambridge University Press, 2018.

Independent Commission on International Development Issues. *North–South, a Programme for Survival: Report of the Independent Commission on International Development Issues.* Cambridge, MA: MIT Press, 1980.

Jensen, Steven L. B. *The Making of International Human Rights: The 1960s, Decolonization and the Reconstruction of Global Values.* Cambridge: Cambridge University Press, 2016.

Johnston, David. *A Brief History of Justice.* Chichester: Wiley-Blackwell, 2011.

Kaufman, Edy. "Prisoners of Conscience: The Shaping of a New Human Rights Concept." *Human Rights Quarterly* 13, no. 3 (1991): 339–367.

Keck, Margaret, and Kathryn Sikkink. *Activists beyond Borders*. Ithaca, NY: Cornell University Press, 1998.

Kim, Hunjoon, and Kathryn Sikkink. "Explaining the Deterrence Effect of Human Rights Prosecutions for Transitional Countries." *International Studies Quarterly* 54, no. 4 (2010): 939–963.

Kim, Junhyup. "To Give or to Act? The Transition of NGOs from Aid Donors to Human Rights Advocates." PhD dissertation, Purdue University, 2018.

Kindornay, Shannon, James Ron, and Charli Carpenter. "Rights-Based Approaches to Development: Implications for NGOs." *Human Rights Quarterly* 34, no. 2 (2012): 472–506.

Klinjsma, Hans-Paul, and Caspar Schweigman. "Country Report: Netherlands." In *Humanitarian Development Studies in Europe*, edited by Julia González, Wilhelm Löwenstein, and Mo Malek, 193–200. Bilbao: University of Deusto, 1999.

Kornbluh, Peter. "Brazil: Torture Techniques Revealed in Declassified U.S. Documents" (July 8, 2014). National Security Archive, George Washington University. https://nsarchive2.gwu.edu/NSAEBB/NSAEBB478/.

Land, Molly K., and Jay D. Aronson. "Human Rights and Technology: New Challenges for Justice and Accountability." *Annual Review of Law and Social Science* 16 (2020): 223–240.

Land, Molly K., and Jay D. Aronson, eds. *New Technologies for Human Rights Law and Practice*. Cambridge: Cambridge University Press, 2018.

Lomax, Michele. "Jara Tribute to Feature Joan Baez." *San Francisco Examiner*, May 27, 1974.

"Luke 10: 25–35: Parable of the Good Samaritan." In *Holy Bible, New Revised Standard Version*. New York: American Bible Society, 1989.

Magrath, Bronwen. "Global Norms, Organisational Change: Framing the Rights-Based Approach at ActionAid." *Third World Quarterly* 35, no. 7 (2014): 1273–1289.

McVeigh, Karen. "Oxfam Funding Crisis Puts 200 UK Jobs at Risk." *The Guardian*, June 4, 2020.

Merry, Sally Engle. *Human Rights and Gender Violence: Translating International Law into Local Justice*. Chicago: University of Chicago Press, 2006.

Minow, Martha. *Upstanders, Whistle-Blowers, and Rescuers*. Koningsberger Lecture, delivered on December 13, 2014, University of Utrecht. The Hague: Eleven International Publishing, 2016.

Montanaro, Laura. *Who Elected Oxfam? A Democratic Defense of Self-appointed Representatives*. Cambridge: Cambridge University Press, 2018.

Moyn, Samuel. *The Last Utopia: Human Rights in History*. Cambridge, MA: Belknap Press of Harvard University Press, 2010.

Moyn, Samuel. *Not Enough: Human Rights in an Unequal World*. Cambridge, MA: Belknap Press of Harvard University Press, 2018.

Neier, Aryeh. "Human Rights Watch." In *The International Human Rights Movement: A History*, 204–232. Princeton, NJ: Princeton University Press, 2012.

Nelson, Paul J., and Ellen Dorsey. *New Rights Advocacy: Changing Strategies of Development and Human Rights NGOs*. Washington, DC: Georgetown University Press, 2008.

Nelson, Paul J., and Ellen Dorsey. "Who Practices Rights-Based Development? A Progress Report on Work at the Nexus of Human Rights and Development." *World Development* 104 (2018): 97–107.

O'Neill, Onora. "Agents of Justice." *Metaphilosophy* 32, no. 1/2 (2001): 180–195.

O'Neill, Onora. "The Dark Side of Human Rights." *International Affairs* 81, no. 2 (2005): 427–439.

O'Neill, Onora. "Who Can Endeavour Peace?" *Canadian Journal of Philosophy* 16, no. supp. 1 (1986): 41–73.

Offenheiser, Raymond C., and Susan H. Holcombe. "Challenges and Opportunities in Implementing a Rights-Based Approach to Development: An Oxfam America Perspective." *Nonprofit and Voluntary Sector Quarterly* 32, no. 2 (2003): 268–306.

Oliner, Samuel P., and Pearl M. Oliner. *The Altruistic Personality: Rescuers of Jews in Nazi Europe*. New York: Free Press, 1988.

Oliver, Myrna. "Ginetta Sagan Dies; Torture Victim Fought for Political Prisoners." *Los Angeles Times*, August 30, 2000.

Onderwater, J. J. M. *Working for Development: An Enquiry into the Potential Need for University Training Programmes in Development Projects.*

Groningen: Pro Human Project, Office for International Cooperation, University of Groningen, 1997.

Oxfam America. "Audited Financial Statements and Form 990: Federal Form 990-2018." https://webassets.oxfamamerica.org/media/documents/OXFA M_AMERICA_INC_-_2018_990.pdf?_gl=1*1x3uwh7*_ga*MTIoNTg2Mjc4 NC4xNjI2ODDAyNzM3*_ga_R58YETD6XK*MTYyNjgwMjczNy4xLjAuMT YyNjgwMjc2Ny4w.

Oxfam America. *Annual Report*. Boston: Oxfam America, 1998.

Oxfam GB. *Annual Review, 1981–82*. Oxford: Oxfam GB, 1982.

Oxfam GB. "Copenhagen Summit: Fine Words, Shame About the Action." *Oxfam Campaigner* no. 15 (Summer 1995): 1.

Oxfam GB. "Oxfam Launches Global Campaign." *Oxfam Campaigner* no. 16 (Autumn 1995): 1.

Oxfam GB. "Social Development Summit." In *The Big Idea: The Newsletter for Oxfam's New Campaign, issue no. 4*. MS. Oxfam CPN/8/5. Folder 4. Oxford: Oxford University, Bodleian Library (September 29, 1994).

Oxfam GB. "'Together for Rights, Together against Poverty,' an Agenda for Equality: Oxfam at the Beijing Women's Conference." *Oxfam Campaigner* no. 16 (Autumn 1995): 2.

Oxfam GB. "'Together for Rights, Together against Poverty,' Southern Launches: Demands of the Poor Should Be Heard." *Oxfam Campaigner* no. 16 (Autumn 1995): 2.

Oxfam GB. "Welcome to *the Big Idea*." In *The Big Idea: The Newsletter for Oxfam's New Campaign, issue no. 1 (1994)*. MS. Oxfam CPN/8/5. Folder 4. Oxford: Oxford University, Bodleian Library (1994).

Oxfam International. *Fighting Inequality to Beat Poverty, Annual Report, 2018–19*. Oxford: Oxfam International, 2019.

Oxfam International. "International Division, Strategic Plan 1999–2004," circa 1995. Oxford: Oxford University, Bodleian Library, MS. Oxfam PRG/2/1/1.

Oxfam International. *Oxfam Annual Report, April 2017–March 2018*. Oxford: Oxfam International, 2019.

Oxfam International. "Oxfam International's Mission." In *Towards Global Equity: Strategic Plan 2001–2004*. Oxford: Oxfam International, 2001. Adopted by the Board of Oxfam International, Ottawa 1996.

Oxfam International. *Towards Global Equity: Strategic Plan, 2001–2004.* Oxford: Oxfam International, 2001.

Oxfam Novib. *Annual Report 2018–19.* The Hague: Oxfam Novib, 2020.

Pallas, Christopher L., and Elizabeth A. Bloodgood, eds. *Beyond the Boomerang: New Patterns in Transcalar Advocacy.* Tuscaloosa: University of Alabama Press, forthcoming.

Price, Richard. "Reversing the Gun Sights: Transnational Civil Society Targets Land Mines." *International Organization* 52, no. 3 (1998): 613–644.

Rawls, John. *The Law of Peoples.* Cambridge, MA: Harvard University Press, 1999.

Rawls, John. *A Theory of Justice.* Cambridge, MA: Belknap Press of Harvard University Press, 1971.

Reus-Smit, Christian. *Individual Rights and the Making of the International System.* Cambridge: Cambridge University Press, 2013.

Reus-Smit, Christian. "On Rights and Institutions." In *Global Basic Rights*, edited by Charles R. Beitz and Robert E. Goodin, 25–48. Oxford: Oxford University Press, 2009.

Risse, Thomas. "'Let's Argue!': Communicative Action in World Politics." *International Organization* 54, no. 1 (Winter 2000): 1–39.

Risse, Thomas, Steven C. Ropp, and Kathryn Sikkink, eds. *The Persistent Power of Human Rights: From Commitment to Compliance.* Cambridge: Cambridge University Press, 2013.

Risse, Thomas, Stephen C. Ropp, and Kathryn Sikkink, eds. *The Power of Human Rights: International Norms and Domestic Change.* Cambridge: Cambridge University Press, 1999.

Rochat, François, and Andre Modigliani. "The Ordinary Quality of Resistance: From Milgram's Laboratory to the Village of Le Chambon." *Journal of Social Issues* 51, no. 3 (1995): 195–210.

Roth, Kenneth. "The Abusers' Reaction: Intensifying Attacks on Human Rights Defenders, Organizations, and Institutions." *Brown Journal of World Affairs* 16, no. 2 (Spring/Summer 2010): 15–26.

Roth, Kenneth. "Defending Economic, Social and Cultural Rights: Practical Issues Faced by an International Human Rights Organization." *Human Rights Quarterly* 26, no. 1 (2004): 63–73.

Royal Geographical Society. *The Global North/South Divide*. London: Royal Geographical Society. www.rgs.org/CMSPages/GetFile.aspx?node guid=9c1ce781-9117-4741-afoa-a6a8b75f32b4&lang=en-GB.

Rubenstein, Jennifer. *Between Samaritans and States: The Political Ethics of Humanitarian NGOs*. Oxford: Oxford University Press, 2015.

Sano, Hans-Otto. "Development and Human Rights: The Necessary, but Partial Integration of Human Rights and Development." *Human Rights Quarterly* 22, no. 3 (2000): 734–752.

Scarry, Elaine. *Thinking in an Emergency*. New York: W. W. Norton, 2011.

Schmitz, Hans Peter, J. Michael Dedmon, Tosca Bruno-van Vijfeijken, and Jaclyn Mahoney. "Democratizing Advocacy?: How Digital Tools Shape International Non-governmental Activism." *Journal of Information Technology & Politics* 17, no. 2 (2020): 174–191.

Scott, Esther. *Oxfam America: Becoming a Global Campaigning Organization*. Cambridge, MA: Harvard Kennedy School, 2004.

Sen, Amartya. *Development as Freedom*. Oxford: Oxford University Press, 1999.

Sen, Amartya. "Freedoms and Needs." New Republic, January 1994, 31–38.

Sen, Amartya. *The Idea of Justice*. Cambridge, MA: Belknap Press of Harvard University Press, 2009.

Shue, Henry. *Basic Rights: Subsistence, Affluence, and U.S. Foreign Policy*. Princeton, NJ: Princeton University Press, 1980.

Sikkink, Kathryn. *Evidence for Hope: Making Human Rights Work in the 21st Century*. Princeton, NJ: Princeton University Press, 2017.

Sikkink, Kathryn. "Human Rights, Principled Issue-Networks, and Sovereignty in Latin America." *International Organization* 47, no. 3 (Summer 1993): 411–441.

Sikkink, Kathryn. *The Justice Cascade: How Human Rights Prosecutions Are Changing World Politics*. New York: W. W. Norton, 2011.

Simmons, Beth. *Mobilizing for Human Rights: International Law in Domestic Politics*. Cambridge: Cambridge University Press, 2009.

Simmons, Beth A., and Anton Strezhnev. "Human Rights and Human Welfare: Looking for a 'Dark Side' to International Law." In *Human Rights Futures*, edited by Stephen Hopgood, Jack Snyder, and Leslie Vinjamuri, 60–87. Cambridge: Cambridge University Press, 2017.

Simmons, Pat. "The Oxfam Global Charter for Basic Rights." In *Words into Action: Basic Rights and the Campaign against World Poverty*, 5. Oxford: Oxfam UK and Ireland, 1995.

Simmons, Pat. *Words into Action: Basic Rights and the Campaign against World Poverty*. Oxford: Oxfam UK and Ireland, 1995.

Smith, Jackie. "Domesticating International Human Rights Norms." In *Social Movements for Global Democracy*, 158–176. Baltimore: Johns Hopkins University Press, 2008.

Smith, Jackie. "Responding to Globalization and Urban Conflict: Human Rights City Initiatives." *Studies in Social Justice* 11, no. 2 (2017): 347–368.

Snyder, Jack. "Empowering Rights through Mass Movements, Religion, and Reform Parties." In *Human Rights Futures*, edited by Stephen Hopgood, Jack Snyder, and Leslie Vinjamuri, 88–113. Cambridge: Cambridge University Press, 2017.

Srivastava, Swati. "Navigating NGO–Government Relations in Human Rights: New Archival Evidence from Amnesty International, 1961–1986." *International Studies Quarterly* (2021), published online, February 18, 2021.

Staub, Ervin. "Preventing Violence and Promoting Active Bystandership and Peace: My Life in Research and Applications." *Peace and Conflict: Journal of Peace Psychology* 24, no. 1 (2018): 95–111.

Staub, Ervin. "The Psychology of Bystanders, Perpetrators, and Heroic Helpers." In *The Psychology of Good and Evil: Why Children, Adults, and Groups Help and Harm Others*, edited by Ervin Staub, 291–324. Cambridge: Cambridge University Press, 2003.

Stroup, Sarah S. *Borders among Activists: International NGOs in the United States, Britain, and France*. Ithaca, NY: Cornell University Press, 2012.

Stroup, Sarah S., and Amanda Murdie. "There's No Place Like Home: Explaining International NGO Advocacy." *The Review of International Organizations* 7, no. 4 (2012): 425–448.

Stroup, Sarah S., and Wendy H. Wong. *The Authority Trap: Strategic Choices of International NGOs*. Ithaca, NY: Cornell University Press, 2017.

Suárez-Krabbe, Julia. "Democratising Democracy, Humanising Human Rights: European Decolonial Social Movements and the 'Alternative Thinking of Alternatives.'" *Migration Letters* 10, no. 3 (2013): 333–341.

Suárez-Krabbe, Julia. "The Other Side of the Story: Human Rights, Race and Gender from a Transatlantic Perspective." In *Decolonizing Enlightenment: Transnational Justice, Human Rights and Democracy in a Postcolonial World*, edited by Nikita Dhawan, 211–226. Opladen: Barbara Budrich, 2014.

Suárez-Krabbe, Julia. "Race, Social Struggles and 'Human' Rights: Contributions from the Global South." In *Europe and the Americas: Transatlantic Approaches to Human Rights*, edited by Erik André Andersen and Eva Maria Lassen, 41–52. Leiden: Brill Nijhoff, 2015.

Thalhammer, Kristina E., Paula O'Laughlin, Myron Peretz Glazer, et al. *Courageous Resistance: The Power of Ordinary People*. New York: Palgrave Macmillan, 2007.

Theis, Joachim. *Promoting Rights-Based Approaches: Experiences from Asia and the Pacific*. Stockholm: Save the Children, 2004. https://archive.crin.org /en/docs/resources/publications/hrbap/promoting.pdf.

Thucydides. *Complete Writings: The Peloponnesian War*, translated by Richard Crawley. New York: Modern Library, 1951.

UN Office of the High Commissioner for Human Rights. "Statement on Visit to the USA, by Professor Philip Alston, United Nations Special Rapporteur on Extreme Poverty and Human Rights" (December 15, 2017). www.ohchr.org/ EN/NewsEvents/Pages/DisplayNews.aspx?NewsID=22533&LangID=E.

UN Special Rapporteur on the Situation of Human Rights Defenders, Mary Lawlor. "Summary." Report on the Priorities of the Mandate of Special Rapporteur to the General Assembly at Its 75th Session (July 16, 2020). UN document no. A/75/165. www.ohchr.org/EN/Issues/SRHRDefenders/Pages/ priorities-sr.aspx.

Uvin, Peter. "From the Right to Development to the Rights-Based Approach: How 'Human Rights' Entered Development." *Development in Practice* 17, no. 4/5 (2007): 597–606.

Valentini, Laura. "Ideal vs. Non-ideal Theory: A Conceptual Map." *Philosophy Compass* 7, no. 9 (2012): 654–664.

Valentini, Laura. "In What Sense Are Human Rights Political? A Preliminary Exploration." *Political Studies* 60 (2012): 180–194.

Wald, Elijah. "Te Recuerdo Amanda." Old Friends: A Songobiography. songblog, August 27, 2016. www.elijahwald.com/songblog/te-recuerdo-amanda/.

Watkins, Kevin, and Oxfam GB. *The Oxfam Education Report*. Oxford: Oxfam GB, 2000.

Watkins, Kevin, and Oxfam GB. *The Oxfam Poverty Report*. Oxford: Oxfam GB, 1995.

White, James Boyd. "The Dissolution of Meaning: Thucydides' History of His World." In *When Words Lose Their Meaning: Constitutions and Reconstitutions of Language, Character, and Community*, 59–92. Chicago: University of Chicago Press, 1984.

White, James Boyd. *Justice as Translation: An Essay in Cultural and Legal Criticism*. Chicago: University of Chicago Press, 1990.

White, James Boyd. "A Way of Reading." In *When Words Lose Their Meaning: Constitutions and Reconstitutions of Language, Character, and Community*, 3–23. Chicago: University of Chicago Press, 1984.

Winkler, Inga T., and Carmel Williams. "The Sustainable Development Goals and Human Rights: A Critical Early Review." *The International Journal of Human Rights* 21, no. 8 (2017): 1023–1028.

Wong, Wendy H. *Internal Affairs: How the Structure of NGOs Transforms Human Rights*. Ithaca, NY: Cornell University Press, 2012.

Wong, Wendy H., Ron Levi, and Julia Deutsch. "Domesticating the Field: The Ford Foundation and the Development of International Human Rights." In *Professional Networks in Transnational Governance*, edited by Leonard Seabrooke and Lasse Folke Henriksen, 82–100. Cambridge: Cambridge University Press, 2017.

Yeginsu, Ceylan. "U.K. Austerity Has Inflicted 'Great Misery,' U.N. Official Says." *New York Times*, May 22, 2019.

Young, John. "Brazilian Torture Cases." *Times*, March 24, 1971.

Ypi, Lea. *Global Justice and Avant-Garde Political Agency*. Oxford: Oxford University Press, 2012.

CPSIA information can be obtained
at www.ICGtesting.com
Printed in the USA
LVHW081651100422
715812LV00012B/1560